PATHWAYS
TO FULFILLMENT

A Life Coach's Guide to Self-Discovery

JJ SNIPES · COLLY GRAHAM · MONIKA SAŁACH · DONNA MCGOFF
JONATHAN EVANS · VICTORIA IVCHENKO · CARLA HARDING · SELBIA LEON
GHAZAL EMAMBAKHSH · TUOMO VAUHKONEN · JACQUI POWER · INARA DODHIYA
PETER MCGEE · MARK DICKSON · SHARON PIEL · CHRIS WILKINSON

Table of Contents

The Importance of Self-Discovery and Understanding the Self in a Fast-Paced World

By JJ Snipes

Introduction

Ever feel lost in a world that won't stop buzzing with notifications, updates, and constant noise? In the middle of all this, finding out who you truly are might just be the most important thing you can do. This chapter seeks to illuminate the importance of getting to know yourself amidst the chaos of everyday life.

Discovering who you really are is like taking a journey through your own story. It's about digging into your thoughts, feelings, and beliefs to uncover what makes you tick. Picture peeling back layers to reveal the experiences that have shaped you, both the good and the tough stuff. This journey involves looking at your strengths and weaknesses, figuring out what matters most to you, and understanding what you want out of life. It's like an ongoing adventure where you learn more about yourself, grow as a person, and connect with the real you. It's a bit like having a personal roadmap to navigate life.

By the end, you'll grasp why delving into the depths of your psyche is not just an esoteric pursuit, but a necessity for true well-being and growth.

Email Overload

The constant influx of emails can interrupt workflow and shift attention away from important tasks.

Online Streaming Services

The availability of endless entertainment options on platforms like Netflix, Hulu, and YouTube can lead to binge-watching and time-wasting.

Gaming

Video games, both on consoles and mobile devices, can be highly immersive and time-consuming, diverting attention from real-world responsibilities.

Always Being Online: Navigating the Smartphone and Social Media Jungle

In a world where smartphones are practically an extension of our hands and social media is the virtual playground we never leave, the constant barrage of notifications, messages, and the tempting allure of various platforms can turn our attention away from what truly matters.

The Smartphone Struggle:

Our smartphones are incredible tools that connect us to the world, but they also have a sneaky way of stealing our focus. The endless ping of notifications can disrupt a productive work session or even a meaningful conversation with a friend. It's like having a tiny, demanding companion that constantly tugs at our sleeve, vying for attention.

Social Media's Allure:

Social media platforms promise connection and entertainment, but they can easily become time-consuming black holes. Scrolling through endless feeds can feel like a never-ending loop, where hours slip away unnoticed. The curated highlight reels of others can also trigger feelings of inadequacy or the pressure to conform to an idealized version of life.

Noise and Overstimulation

Urban environments with constant noise, visual stimuli, and information overload can contribute to distraction and reduced concentration.

Instant Messaging Apps

Apps like WhatsApp and Messenger provide immediate communication, but can also be a source of distraction when not managed properly.

News and Information Overload

The 24/7 news cycle, coupled with the abundance of information on the internet, can be overwhelming and distract individuals from their daily tasks.

Workplace Distractions

Open office environments, frequent meetings, and constant collaboration can disrupt workflow and hinder productivity.

With our phones always in our hands, we're connected to everything and everyone. This can be fun and helpful, but it can also make it hard for us to hear our own thoughts. **Growing up in the 70's and 80's there were no cell phones**. My challenge to you. Leave all phones at home for a day. Take your partner/ family or just yourself and go out for a few hours. Come out of the rat race. Embrace life without the electronic crutches of today's society and **find yourself**. Believe me it will be refreshing.

Trying to Fit In: The Social Media Conundrum

In the captivating realm of social media, where filters turn ordinary moments into dazzling spectacles and everyone seems to be leading a life of perpetual bliss, the pressure to fit in and measure up to an unrealistic standard can be overwhelming.

The Picture-Perfect Illusion:

Scrolling through social media feeds often feels like flipping through the glossy pages of a magazine dedicated to flawless lives. Each post presents a carefully curated snapshot, showcasing moments of joy, success, and seemingly unattainable perfection. These images create an illusion of an ideal life—one filled with constant excitement, flawless relationships, and unending success.

The Myth of Perfection:

Challenge the notion that perfection is attainable or even desirable. Imperfections and vulnerabilities make individuals unique and relatable.

Discover the importance of self-acceptance and self-love, acknowledge and embrace flaws as part of the human experience.

I have come to the realization that people would rather live in a fantasy world than reality. I help my clients realize that another person's opinion of them is none of their business. Not everyone is going to like you and you sure can't please everyone either. Embrace your authenticity and keep moving forward.

The Power of Self-Validation:

I Encourage individuals to derive validation from within rather than relying solely on external sources.

Explore techniques for self-reflection, recognizing personal achievements, and celebrating individual strengths.

Why Self-Discovery Matters

Finding Purpose:

The journey of self-discovery is a crucial aspect of unlocking one's purpose in life. It involves delving deep into the intricate layers of one's personality to unravel values, passions, and strengths. This profound understanding becomes a guiding light, influencing critical life decisions ranging from career choices to the dynamics of personal relationships. By aligning one's path with their authentic self, individuals embark on a journey that resonates with their innermost desires, fostering a sense of purpose and fulfillment.

Emotional Well-Being:

A profound knowledge of oneself forms the cornerstone of emotional intelligence, enabling individuals to navigate the complex landscape of their emotions with finesse. This self-awareness equips them to identify triggers, establish personal boundaries, and develop effective strategies to cope with life's inevitable challenges, such as stress and anxiety. Recognizing that the ups and downs are part of a universal journey shared by people from all walks of life, irrespective of social status, serves as a comforting reminder that everyone faces hurdles on their path.

Empowered Decisions:

Individuals who are in tune with their inner selves possess a unique power—the ability to make decisions that resonate with their true desires. This empowerment is transformative, leading to a life filled with more authentic and fulfilling experiences, while minimizing the likelihood of regrets. The decisions made from a place of self-awareness carry a deeper sense of purpose and alignment with one's values, resulting in a more meaningful and intentional existence.

Introspection and Reflection:

At the heart of self-discovery lies the art of introspection and reflection. Taking moments of solitude to ponder, whether through writing down thoughts, engaging in meditation, or simply daydreaming, is a vital practice. These introspective moments provide a sanctuary for individuals to genuinely look within, unveiling the nuances of their thoughts, feelings, and aspirations.

Seek Feedback from Trusted Friends:

In the pursuit of self-discovery, the perspective of trusted friends becomes a valuable asset. Engaging in meaningful conversations with those who know us well can offer insights that might be elusive to our own perception. Honest feedback from friends acts as a mirror, reflecting aspects of ourselves that we may not have consciously recognized. This external perspective contributes to a more holistic understanding of who we are, enriching the self-discovery journey.

Real-life Stories

Maya's Transformative Expedition:

Maya, a seasoned 29-year-old software engineer, found herself ensnared in the daily grind of a thriving tech career. Despite external success, a sense of fulfillment eluded her. In search of deeper meaning, she made a bold decision to embark on a transformative journey. Taking a hiatus from her demanding job, Maya set out to explore the world, hoping to unravel the intricate tapestry of her own aspirations.

During her travels, Maya serendipitously found herself in the picturesque landscapes of Nepal. Intrigued by the local culture and inspired by a profound sense of purpose, she decided to dedicate her time to volunteering at a humble school nestled within the heart of the community. The experience proved to be nothing short of revelatory for Maya, as she discovered a profound joy and fulfillment in nurturing young minds.

The resonance between Maya and her newfound passion was undeniable. Overwhelmed by the sense of purpose she found in education; Maya resolved to forge a new path for herself. She made the courageous decision to transition from the fast-paced world of technology to the more emotionally rewarding realm of education, thereby embarking on a career that aligned with her authentic self.

Tom's Cathartic Awakening:

In a bustling corporate environment, Tom found himself grappling with a recurring issue that had started to affect both his professional and personal life—uncontrollable bursts of anger. After a particularly heated argument at work, Tom recognized the imperative need for a profound shift in his approach to managing emotions.

In a proactive pursuit of self-improvement, Tom sought therapy as a means of unravelling the complex layers of his emotional turmoil. Through introspective sessions and guided self-exploration, he unearthed unresolved issues from his childhood that had been silently fueling his temperamental outbursts. Tom's revelation marked the inception of a transformative journey toward understanding and healing.

Acknowledging the deep-seated roots of his anger allowed Tom to confront and make peace with the past. Armed with newfound self-awareness, he developed coping mechanisms and strategies to manage his emotional responses effectively. This transformative process not only mended professional relationships but also fostered personal growth, enabling Tom to navigate the complexities of life with a newfound sense of emotional resilience and balance.

Conclusion:

In the midst of life's chaotic hustle, finding solace in self-reflection becomes crucial. Begin the journey of self-discovery today; even a small introspective step yields profound results. Embracing self-awareness empowers you to navigate the complexities of the world with clarity and purpose. Listen to your inner voice—it holds the key to understanding and thriving in this unpredictable journey called life.

CHAPTER 2

The Role of a Life Coach in your Journey

By Colly Graham

A coach is a vehicle to take you from where you are to where you want to go on your journey through life. The role of a life coach on your journey through life is to be your partner, mentor, and a cheerleader.

However, many people are seeking to travel in the wrong direction, and the role of the coach is to turn you around and point you in the right direction and, of course, help you get there.

What are your goals in life? Here's an exercise I want you to do right now, take out your journal. Maybe you don't have a journal, or perhaps you do. If you already journal, well done. If you haven't journaled, it's the ideal tool to help you get on track to get where you want to be. I ask, no, I beg you to get a journal. Some of the most influential people in history kept journals, including Charles Darwin, Marie Curie, Thomas Edison.

Journaling can help you set realistic and achievable goals that are practical, realistic, attainable, measurable, known and understood. (PRAMKU). You can then use your journal to break down your big goals into smaller more manageable steps, and to assign deadlines and milestones for each step. This can help you stay focused, organized, and motivated, and to track your progress and results.

Journaling is a simple and powerful way to improve your mental, emotional, and physical health. It can also help you to unleash your creativity, enhance your memory, and discover yourself.

Make notes in your journal of what you want from life. In this chapter I will discuss later how journaling will help you create the life you want. I encourage you to start journaling today.

Hierarchy of Needs

What do you want on your life's journey? As a coach it's my role to help you get there. Let us, at this point, consider Maslow's hierarchy of needs as a foundation for discovering what you need in your life.

Maslow's hierarchy of needs is a theory that establishes the needs all human beings have, developed with a ladder of importance. The fulfilment of these needs helps to dictate a person's individual behaviors and include physiological, safety, love and belonging, esteem, and self-actualization.

The most basic of needs and one that must be fulfilled before the rest are physiological needs. This includes needs such as food, clothing, air, water, and warmth that ensures physical health are included in this category.

Safety needs come next in this hierarchy. These needs focus on stability, security and a protection from harms that are both physical and emotional in nature.

Love and belonging needs revolve around your need for emotional and personal relationships, community, and connectedness. It also includes the need for friendship, experiencing affection, and intimacy.

Self-esteem needs is the need to have confidence, competence, achievement, mastery, independence, and freedom. This is the need to feel good about oneself and one's abilities, and to be proud of one's accomplishments.

Self-actualisation needs refer to the discovery of your potential, self-fulfillment, the seeking of personal ad-vancement, and fulfilling experiences. This level of need revolves around the understanding of the self, including your capabilities and potential.

One may describe self-actualisation as enlightenment. Enlightenment can be described as the pursuit of personal and social happiness, and the cultivation of moral and aesthetic values.

Often the goals we seek on our journey through life is based in the pursuit of happiness. In a nutshell we are seeking that which will make us happy.

Here are some of the key ideas my friend Robert Holden teaches about happiness that resonate with me. Happiness is not something you get, but something you are. Happiness is your true nature, and it's always available to you, regardless of your circumstances. Happiness is not dependent on external factors, such as money, success, or relationships, but on your inner state of mind and heart.

Happiness is a choice; you can choose to be happy or unhappy in any moment, by choosing your thoughts, feelings, and actions. You can also choose to be happy for no reason, by simply being grateful, present, and authentic.

Contentment can enhance happiness, but it doesn't guarantee it. Contentment can help us appreciate what we have, live in the present moment, and cope with challenges and difficulties. Contentment can also reduce our cravings, expectations, and comparisons that may cause us to feel unhappy or dissatisfied. However, contentment does not mean that we never experience negative emotions, such as sadness, anger, or fear. Contentment also does not mean that we stop pursuing our goals, dreams, and passions.

Happiness and contentment are not destinations, but a journey, and you can enjoy every step of the way.

Back to your journal, what are you now seeking to achieve? What are your goals? Where do you want to be? Goals fall into seven areas:

Career

This area of goal relates to your professional development, such as advancing your skills, education, position, income, or impact in your chosen field. Some examples of career goals include excelling in your current job, finding a new more fulfilling job, starting a business, or getting a qualification.

Finance

This area of goal relates to your financial management, such as increasing your income, saving, investing, budgeting, or paying off debt. Examples of financial goals are saving for retirement, buying a house, becoming debt-free, or creating an emergency fund.

Health

This area of goal relates to your physical and mental well-being, such as improving your fitness, nutrition, sleep, or mood. Some examples of health goals are losing weight, quitting smoking, running a marathon, or meditating daily.

Leisure

This area of goal relates to your hobbies, interests, and passions, such as learning a new skill, pursuing a creative project, traveling, or having fun. Some examples of leisure goals are learning a foreign language, writing a book, visiting a new country, or playing an instrument.

Organisation

This area of goal relates to your productivity, efficiency, and orderliness, such as managing your time, tasks, space, or resources. Some examples of organization goals are decluttering your home, creating a morning routine, using a planner, or automating your bills.

Relationships

This area of goal relates to your social and emotional connections, such as building, maintaining, or enhancing your relationships with your family, friends, partner, or community. Some examples of relationship goals are making time more time for those that you love, forging new friendships, finding a romantic partner, or joining a club.

Spirituality

This area of goal relates to your personal growth, meaning, and purpose, such as exploring your beliefs, values, and identity, or connecting with something greater than yourself. Some examples of spirituality goals are reading a religious text, attending a service, volunteering, or practicing gratitude.

Having set your goals in the seven areas of your life; Career, Finance, Health, Leisure, Organisation, Relationships and Spirituality; ask yourself are these goals practical, realistic, attainable, known and understood?

Once you answer the above questions ask yourself, *why do I want these goals and what will they do for me?*

Following these questions, you may wish or want to refine your goals, which is perfectly fine.

The Four Pillars of Wealth

How will coaching help you achieve your goals? There are four areas of your life where your coach will take you on your journey to achieve your goals. Mark Walden and Chris Manning in their book NeuroWisdom describe these four areas as the four pillars of wealth. As a coach I view them as the four pillars of success. The four pillars are Motivation, Decision Making, Creativity and Awareness.

Motivation

Motivation is the desire, curiosity, and pleasure propelling individuals towards self-discovery, achievement, and fulfilment. Motivation serves as the driving force behind our actions, compelling us to set and pursue goals, overcome challenges, and reach new heights.

Desire, akin to a magnetic force, draws us towards our aspirations and dreams. Curiosity is the insatiable hunger for knowledge and understanding, it's the engine of intellectual exploration. It propels us to question, learn, and innovate, fostering a continuous cycle of discovery.

Pleasure is the sweet reward of our efforts, provides the emotional satisfaction that reinforces positive behavior. Whether fuelled by external rewards or intrinsic passion, motivation is the spark that ignites our ambition and propels us forward on the path to achieve our goals and success.

Decision Making

Decision Making transforms the abstract desire of motivation into concrete plans and strategies, enabling us to navigate the complex journey towards our goals. Motivation, as a powerful driving force, may set the stage, but it's through thoughtful decision-making that aspirations are translated into actionable steps. Decision-making involves evaluating various options, considering potential outcomes, and choosing the most effective course of action to align with our objectives.

The process of decision-making empowers us to break down our goals into manageable tasks and prioritize actions based on their significance and feasibility. It requires a blend of critical thinking, foresight, and a deep understanding of our motivations. Decisions act as the bridge between motivation and implementation.

Creativity

Creativity becomes a natural and potent ally in the journey from decision-making to goal attainment. Once decisions are made and plans are set, creativity steps in as the driving force that infuses innovation, adaptability, and originality into the execution of those plans. Decision-making lays the groundwork, establishing a framework within which creativity can flourish. It provides the structure and direction, and creativity adds the flair, allowing for a dynamic and responsive approach to achieving goals.

Creativity often taps into the wellspring of intuition, drawing from an individual's deep reservoir of experiences, emotions, and tacit knowledge. Intuition serves as a silent guide, providing a sense of direction or suggesting unconventional approaches that might not be immediately apparent through logical analysis alone. In creative endeavors, intuitive insights can lead to the discovery of groundbreaking concepts or the formulation of artistic expressions that defy conventional norms.

How The Life Coach Guides You

The life coach on your journey will help you discover that all your answers are inside yourself. A life coach serves as a guiding companion on your personal journey, illuminating the path to self-discovery and empowerment. One of the profound insights they often emphasize is the notion that, fundamentally, all the answers you seek are within yourself. This philosophy underscores the belief that individuals possess an innate reservoir of wisdom, intuition, and self-awareness that, when tapped into, can offer valuable guidance for navigating life's challenges and making informed decisions.

The role of the life coach is not to provide ready-made solutions but to facilitate a process of introspection, exploration, and self-realization. Through thoughtful questioning, active listening, and targeted exercises, a life coach helps you uncover your unique strengths, values, and aspirations. They encourage you to delve into your own experiences, beliefs, and emotions to find the insights and solutions that resonate most authentically with who you are. Ultimately, the journey with a life coach becomes a collaborative exploration of the rich terrain within, unveiling the wisdom that can guide you towards a more fulfilling and meaningful life.

i.   https://www.robertholden.com/the-happiness-project/
ii. https://www.goodreads.com/en/book/show/30279521

CHAPTER 3

Key Philosophies in Life Coaching on Self-Discovery

An exploration of dominant coaching theories and practices
By Monika Salach

When we think of coaching, we usually associate it with the concept of self-discovery. After all, helping clients uncover their true potential and achieve their goals is at the heart of any coaching practice.

However, beneath this seemingly simple and general idea of self-discovery coaching lies a world of philosophies and theories that have been developed and refined by experts over the years.

Each coach shapes their own coaching philosophy and approach, utilizing a diverse range of techniques and theories and adjusting them to their unique style and experience. Each coach is always ready to build knowledge and a fuller toolbox for their practice. But before diving into the realm of theories and philosophies of self-discovery coaching let's start with the basics: the definition of a coaching philosophy.

Coaching Philosophy

A coaching philosophy describes principles that the coach uses while coaching a client, and serves as a guide in their professional life, helping them to make informed decisions and to emulate a desired behavior. A coach forms their own coaching philosophy by understanding 3 main aspects of their coaching:

1.) Purpose (Why I got into coaching)
2.) Values (What are my values which I base my coaching on)
3.) Style (How I coach)

Each coach defines their own philosophy, which will be constantly updated as they gain more knowledge, self-awareness, and experience. However, there are some basic coaching values and styles that should be consistent for everyone in this field. This was the foundation that was implanted in our heads, regardless of our differing courses and experiences.

In my opinion, and in the opinion of many coaches I spoke to, the non-negotiable base for developing your own, unique coaching philosophy, can be summarized as follows:

Clients are responsible for their actions and the results they create. We coaches hold an open space for the clients and allow them to lead their discovery, without exposing them to our judgment, biases, and advice. We are there to actively listen, be fully engaged, ask powerful questions, believe in their resourcefulness, hold them accountable, and celebrate with them their successes.

Self-Awareness

Self-awareness is commonly defined as: knowing one's own values, passions, aspirations, talents, weaknesses, and strengths. It's about understanding what you care about, what you're good at, and where you struggle. It also involves recognizing how you react in different situations, handle tough times, and affect the people around you.

There are two sides to self-awareness, internal and external. Internal self-awareness is simply looking inside yourself. It's like having a clear mirror to see your feelings, thoughts, and behaviors, helping you discover who you are, what drives you to feel like your true self, and why you approach challenges, goals, and decisions in a certain way.

External self-awareness, on the other hand, is like looking at a movie that shows how others see you – you are in the audience, watching your own performance. It helps you understand how your actions and words affect people, and is a first step to improve your interactions with others.

Coaching on Self-Awareness

The coaching philosophy explained above introduces values and styles that are appropriate for all forms of coaching. But how should it be extended to facilitate the client's self-discovery?

A client's self-awareness can be its own goal and can be a necessary condition for achieving life or career objectives. To accompany the client on this path, the coach must possess distinct traits and knowledge that usually must exceed that of an average coach.

Coach's Values

It goes without saying that to support clients on their path to self-discovery successfully, the coach must constantly work on their own self-awareness. That self-awareness can then go towards building self-confidence and worth, and eventually towards the discovery of a life purpose. The appreciation of personal and, frequently, spiritual growth makes such a coach uniquely predestined to carry this ideal and share it with other people.

Being patient is one of the crucial values needed in a self-discovery coach. Reaching deeply into themselves can be a long and sometimes painful process for the client, and the coach must understand that any push to speed it up may shut down the client and any opportunity for further reflection.

To foster a client's confidence to introspect, a coach must build trust, create a safe space, and remain non-judgmental.

The client may discover thoughts and emotions that are difficult for them to share, and providing an atmosphere that allows them to open up is a necessary condition to carry the process forward.

The best coaches have faith in their clients' ability to uncover the solutions and achieve the goals on their own. The coach is a partner, who helps the client to go deeper into their emotions and thoughts, and to see themselves and their environment from a different point of view. Additionally, a self-discovery coach has to tactfully suggest the methods and tools that can help the client on the path to their true self.

Coaching Style

There are many coaching styles to choose from, but some are particularly effective at fostering a client's self-awareness. They usually cover both methods to discover the client's true personality manifested in their emotions, thoughts, behaviors; and the processes leading to growth and change. The main styles that we deem most effective are ACT, Appreciative inquiry Coaching, Cognitive Behavioral Coaching, Emotional Intelligence Coaching, and Intentional Change Theory.

Acceptance and Commitment Coaching is an approach based on acceptance and commitment therapy (ACT) principles. It involves guiding individuals to mindfully acknowledge and embrace their challenging emotions, instead of resisting or avoiding them. This process helps clients move beyond these emotions, enabling them to clarify their personal values and goals.

Appreciative Inquiry Coaching is a strengths-based approach that focuses on exploring and magnifying an individual's positive attributes, successes, and what works well in their life. This method seeks to inspire personal growth and change by leveraging the client's existing strengths and highlighting their potential for further development and success.

Cognitive Behavioral Coaching is a set of techniques initiated by guided discoveries to help illuminate a client's thought patterns, emotional life, and behaviors. It leads to an understanding of how their beliefs and perspectives determine and distort their reactions.

In **Emotional Intelligence Coaching** the coach helps the client identify and accept their emotions, understand the unmet needs signaled by unpleasant emotions, and see these as opportunities to learn and grow.

Intentional Change Theory is a five-step leadership coaching model useful for building motivation for self-change. It helps the client discover their vision for their ideal self, understand their current self-compared to their desired future self, and create a learning agenda to achieve this ideal self. This learning agenda creates a roadmap for experimenting with and practicing new habits and getting both social and environmental support. The coach may freely blend techniques from different models or stick to the ones they deem the most successful and natural.

Coaching Tools

With a long history of examining "the self" in philosophies and religions, it's no surprise that there are many methods of building self-awareness, old and new, which are available for the coaches. The methods can be applied individually by the client, used during the coaching session, or serve as a starting point for further exploration. Some of the methods will be described in more detail in the following chapters of the book.

Mindfulness and Meditation (chapter 8)

Meditation and mindfulness practices are very valuable tools for fostering self-awareness and personal development. Meditation enables the client to cultivate focus, reduce stress, and enhance emotional regulation, while mindfulness encourages being fully present in the moment and non-judgmentally observing one's experiences. Mindfulness and meditation help clients become more in tune with their thoughts, emotions, and behaviors, identify limiting beliefs and habits, and develop a deeper understanding of themselves.

Journaling (chapter 7)

Journaling is a highly effective coaching method for raising self-awareness. It involves the practice of regularly writing down one's thoughts, feelings, experiences, and reflections in a dedicated journal or diary. When used in a coaching context, journaling can help individuals gain a deeper understanding of themselves, their emotions, and their thought processes.

By promoting systematic reflection, the client will get clarity and insights, notice a fresh perspective on their challenges and opportunities, or identify patterns in their thoughts, emotions, and behaviors. All these can help them recognize their strengths, weaknesses, triggers, and habits, leading to greater self-awareness.

Uncovering Underlying Beliefs

Underlying beliefs are the deep-seated and often un-conscious factors that shape a person's thoughts, feel-ings, and behaviors. These beliefs are usually formed early in life and are influenced by a combination of personal ex-periences, cultural upbringing, family values, and societal norms. Challenging and altering unhelpful underlying be-liefs with the help of the coach will lead to personal growth, improved self-awareness, and more positive life outcomes.

Wheel of Life

The Wheel of Life can help clients to assess and improve various aspects of their lives. It consists of a circle divided into segments or categories, each representing a different area of a person's life: career, health, relationships, finance, personal growth, friends and family, romance, fun and recreation, and physical environment.

Considering the relative importance of each area, the client is naturally prompted to reflect on the priorities and satisfaction of each aspect of their life.

Personality Assessments

There are many assessments for evaluating personality traits, some better than others. It's important to choose the assessment carefully before recommending it to the client, to make sure it will give them the answers they are looking for. It's also crucial that the coach is familiar with the test and able to interpret and discuss the results with their client. As such assessments are just one of the tools used during self-awareness coaching, they can't be treated independently from all other explorations and reflections that the client is doing.

Here are some examples of personality tests you may want to use with your clients:

1.) Enneagram
2.) Myers-Briggs Type Indicator (MBTI)

3.) Big Five Personality Model

360-Degree Feedback

360-degree feedback is frequently used within companies as a way for managers to get a fuller picture of someone's strengths and weaknesses as opposed to a two-way conversation. Information about an individual is collected from the colleagues who work directly with the person: supervisors, colleagues, direct reports, customers, and vendors.

360-degree feedback can also be used in a coaching context. The questions used should be designed by a client and a coach individually depending on the client's needs, doubts, and areas of special interest. Input provided by friends, family, and colleagues, usually in a written form, help the client to identify how they are perceived by others and identify blind spots in their self-awareness.

Identifying Core Values (chapter 6)

Uncovering a client's values is crucial for them to become aware of what drives them in their lives, and how their idealistic view of themselves correlates with reality. There are multiple methods available, either to be executed during a coaching session, or in the form of an assessment to be taken by the client separately (the results should still be discussed with the coach).

Some Methods for Identifying Core Values

1. Questioning and Self-Reflection during the coaching sessions.
2. Values elicitation exercises where clients generate or select values from a list and prioritize them. It may trigger a coaching conversation on their meaning, related life events, or their impact on decision-making.
3. Discussing role models and inspirations.
4. Exploring cultural, family, and personal background.
5. Guided visualization exercises to help clients imagine their ideal future and the values that would be dominant in that scenario.
6. Values Assessment Tools such as the Schwartz Value Survey.

Strengths Assessments

Strengths assessments allow clients to recognize and harness their strengths and natural abilities. Building upon them, the clients can unlock their full potential, achieve personal and professional goals, and improve overall well-being.

Examples of the Strengths Assessments:

1. StrengthsFinder assessment, which reveals a person's top strengths among a list of 34.

2. VIA Survey of Character Strengths, which assesses 24 character strengths such as kindness, perseverance, and creativity.

3. Clifton Strengths assessment is a widely recognized tool that identifies a person's top five strengths out of 34 possible themes. This assessment can help individuals understand their dominant talents and how to apply them in various aspects of their lives, from career choices to personal relationships.

4. Gallup Strengths-based Leadership assessment focuses on leadership strengths, enabling clients to develop their leadership skills and enhance their performance in leadership roles.

Johari Window Technique

The Johari Window technique can be used by the client in order to understand who they are and how they relate to others. It's represented by four panes defined on 2 dimensions: known/unknown to oneself, and known/unknown to others:

- **Open** – What we and others know about ourselves.
- **Hidden** – What we know about ourselves, but others do not.
- **Blind Spot** – What others know about us, but we do not.
- **Unknown** – What we and others do not know about ourselves.

It may be unclear for the client what to put in the panes initially, but different coaching explorations like 360-Degree Feedback can help to uncover a clearer understanding of the self.

SWOT Analysis

SWOT analysis involves identifying a person's Strengths, Weaknesses, Opportunities, and Threats.

- **Strengths** - Core competencies and talents, which serve as a solid foundation for personal and professional growth.
- **Weaknesses** - Areas that may require improvement, offering a roadmap for personal development.
- **Opportunities** – External factors that could be exploited to your advantage.
- **Threats** -Elements in the environment that could jeopardize a quest for personal development.

One of the primary benefits of the SWOT analysis is its simplicity and versatility. It can be applied to various aspects of a client's life, such as career, relationships, or personal development. By breaking down self-awareness into these four components, clients gain clarity on their internal resources, vulnerabilities, and external circumstances, which empowers them to take charge of their personal and professional growth and make the most of their unique qualities and opportunities while mitigating potential threats to their well-being.

Conclusion

The quest for self-awareness is probably as old as humanity itself. Going back as far as Ancient Greece, we can find Socrates saying that the unexamined life was not worth living.

People look inside themselves to uncover their true strengths, weaknesses, aspirations, emotions, values, passions, and goals. By growing self-awareness, people hope to unlock their potential, boost personal growth, align their actions with their authentic selves, and find a sense of purpose and direction in life.

Self-discovery can be attained by anyone on their own, but coaches are uniquely predestined with their knowledge, experience, and dedication to facilitate it for the clients. Coaches are able to apply appropriate coaching methods and techniques to provide a structured and supportive space for exploration and to empower the clients on their journey. Also, for the coach, taking a client on a journey of self-discovery can be a great privilege and an opportunity for their own self-growth.

CHAPTER 4

The Inner Landscape: Emotions, Thoughts and Beliefs

"A dream is the seed.
Vision plants it.
Imagination nurtures growth.
Opportunities create blooms.
Reflection becomes reality."
By Donna McGoff, Life Coach

When suffering effects of a major personal trauma, we tend to search for distractions and influences outside of ourselves. We look for ways to alleviate our pain. We don't want to be "stuck" but feel there are weeds sprouting up all around us holding us down. The presence of these weeds indicates what we must do next. We can either mow them down to the surface or pull them out at the root and set ourselves free.

Through years of study, experience, and expertise, I've found three simple strategies to incorporate as a practice before taking action to overcome major problems. Integrating these strategies is an inside job. They lead to deeper self-discovery and inner power. When we nurture our inner landscape, we plant the seeds that bear the fruit of a more balanced outer world.

I use these three strategies to help divorced women who feel "stuck" and struggle with moving out of the past to rebuild their lives. The strategies of changing their focus, thinking, and attitude, can help open their minds to the possibility of overriding conflicted feelings and emotions. This can lead to them validating their hopes, dreams, and visions for better results in the future. For each strategy, I give a common example of a past client and part of their personal story so that you can understand how each strategy benefits them.

When we learn to shift our focus from our present reality to the vision of how we want our life to be going forward, we begin to feel hope, energy, and a sense of motivation to begin taking steps in that direction. The more we focus on our vision for the future, the less energy we spend focusing on the past. The more we become aware or conscious of our thinking, the more control and success we will have in achieving goals. The more we cultivate a good attitude, the more cognizant we are of opportunities and possibilities we might otherwise miss. We set ourselves up for success.

Then, seeds replace weeds. When our inner landscape has been properly weeded, we begin to plant seeds for our new life to grow freely and flourish. We see with our heart as our inner landscape changes. We start to believe we can create a life we would love living for the future.

Change Our Focus

When our focus stays the same, our actions stay the same, and we experience the same results over and over. There can be no other way. Wayne Dyer, known as the Father of Motivation, sums it up well, "When you change the way you look at things, the things you look at change."

Emily was devastated to find out that her husband was unfaithful during the marriage. Very gradually over the years, Emily and Thomas had grown apart. Thomas started putting in longer hours at the office, and, as a teacher, Emily became more involved with leading extra-curricular activities at her school.

She admits she had her suspicions but would dismiss the possibility of his cheating from her mind. Emily ignored many of the signs.

One night, Thomas comes home after a long evening at the office. Emily greets him at the door. As she leans in and opens her arms to hug him, she can smell perfume on his shirt that isn't hers.

When she starts digging into the past, she discovers other infidelities. Once divorced, she continues to experience so many conflicted feelings and emotions about it. These conflicted feelings prevent her from moving forward.

Emily has a pity party for whomever will listen, along with playing the victim for all it's worth. Finally, after several years, she begins to discover that playing the victim keeps her stuck in a past that no longer serves her. She is ready to pull out the weeds and plant new seeds that will nourish her inner landscape.

Here's How She Can Do It

Emily needs to ask herself this question: What lesson(s) can I learn from my divorce? The answer(s) she comes up with can help to take the focus off conflicted feelings and negative self-talk. She can replace those thoughts and feelings with the lesson learned or even the good that can be found in the situation. It shifts her focus towards what lesson this situation has for her so that she can avoid attracting it again in the future.

To Emily, it feels counterintuitive at first; but when she takes a closer, deeper look inside the question, she creates space inside her mind to entertain a different perspective.

There is good in every challenging situation. Emily's current focus is what is blocking her progress. There are two sides of a coin. Where there's an up, there has to be a down. If there's an in, there has to be an out. It can be no other way; otherwise, how can we measure whether it's good or bad? We can't measure one without the other.

What Does Emily Discover?

By looking at her situation from a different point of view, Emily realizes that her problem begins and ends with her. She discovers that she has a pattern of attracting emotionally unavailable men. She thought she just had bad luck or an imaginary neon sign on her forehead saying, "Selfish, self-absorbed men are welcome here."

With further introspection, she realizes that all her relationships with men, including her father, are with emotionally unavailable ones.

With this new knowledge and different way of looking at her present situation, she can uproot the weeds. Every time conflicted feelings and negative self-talk rise to the surface, she immediately replaces the self-talk with the lessons she's learned from the experience. It helps her to focus her attention on what she can do now, which immediately takes the focus off the past.

Responding instead of reacting, Emily overrides her conflicted feelings and emotions validating her inner desire to achieve better results. She starts to feel more confidence and respect for herself and develops a cheerful attitude towards life. Now, her focus is on attracting someone with qualities that support a healthy, loving relationship.

Change Our Thoughts

"Triggering Thoughts" cause physical reactions in our body that we don't want but are unaware of how to control.

Lola goes out for a walk on a warm, sunny day. Just up ahead, she sees a happy couple holding hands and walking along with a bounce to their step. From what she can tell from their body language, they're engaged in loving conversation.

Her observation "triggers" longing and discontent as it elicits sad, remorseful thoughts and feelings of loss relating to her own personal experience. The longing and discontent manifest into physical feelings as she associates her observation of the couple with similar, loving memories from her own past.

These physical feelings are irritating and cause physical discomfort. The physical feelings "trigger" Lola to behave out-of-character or impulsive ways. The physical feelings are intense and uncomfortable. She may not even realize the physical feelings are a "trigger" stemming from her association of what she sees, and how they connect to her own feelings and memories. All she wants to do right now is relieve herself of them.

When she feels "triggered" sometimes she experiences a tension headache, dives into the refrigerator, drinks too much wine, or says things she wishes she hadn't. Lola feels desperate to relieve her discomfort, even if it means resorting to unhealthy choices that she will later regret.

This is how unhealthy habits or addictive behaviors can manifest within us. We just want to stop the pain it brings up to the surface.

Lola was the one who initiated the divorce. She married David while he was in law school. She had just finished college. They were high school sweethearts and neither had dated anyone else. For many years, she was deeply in love with him. David was a good husband and a devoted father, and they had many cherished, wonderful memories of their life together.

Subtly over the years, David developed a drinking problem. He didn't drink every day; but when he did, he just couldn't stop. Eventually, his behavior became almost intolerable. She struggled with her decision to get a divorce, and she felt a sense of emptiness and shame for initiating it. It weighed heavily on her heart especially because of the effect it would have on her children.

She avoided making the decision for so long because she didn't want to feel the emotions and judgment this decision was going to create. Although Lola was being true to herself, she struggled with getting divorced, dealing with her "triggering feelings" in an appropriate way.

What if There's a Better Way?

What if Lola can release the uncomfortable, constricted feelings before they take hold? What if she learns how to respond in a way that will not only put her on the path to better results but also give her power and control over her life? What if she learns how to replace a "triggering feeling" with a healthy alternative when she feels it coming on?

Everything begins and ends with our thinking. The more conscious we are of what we think, the more control we have over our destiny. If we haven't developed the strategy of noticing our thoughts; especially the ones that don't serve our higher self, they can control us. Oftentimes, we aren't aware of these thoughts that come sneaking into our mind; and suddenly, we're caught up in negative thinking or scenarios. These thoughts prevent us from focusing on what we can do to overcome our challenges. They keep us stuck in the weeds.

We can learn not to get involved with negative thoughts that bring us down and waste our time and energy. It's the monkey mind or incessant inner chatter that alerts

us to knowing we need to change our thoughts. Self-talk is not thinking.

We can change our thoughts in an instant! If we step on a nail, our body at once alerts us to the pain of it. It's the same with our thoughts, except we can choose to change our thoughts in that moment, while a nail piercing our foot will always hurt. We have no control over that, but we have control over our thinking. It's the one sacred thing that we own and have the power to control.

It's our superpower but many don't realize it.

If we find ourselves dwelling on a bad day or our past mistakes and can't cease the negative conversation happening inside our minds, we can take a moment and acknowledge this reaction. We can begin to have the thought without getting involved with it.

When we first try to learn how to do this, we may not catch the negative thought as we think it. If we don't catch the thought as we think it, we experience an uncomfortable, constricted feeling inside because the negative thought doesn't make us feel good. (It's our physical trigger.)

A triggering thought alerts us to the response that the body has to that thought. The response could be an upset stomach, throat or chest tightening up, sweaty hands, or color rising in our cheeks...

Why Learn to Become Aware Of "Thought Triggers"

Once we're aware of what's going on in our body, we can push the negative or uncomfortable thought aside, replacing it with a positive one. When we can do that, the thought no longer has control over us. Replacing it with an empowering thought or an affirmation works best.

We begin to control our life instead of undesirable feelings and thoughts controlling it. Finally, once we remove the negativity, we make space in our minds to change the way we think about a challenging situation. We're ready to focus on what's positive about it. (Two sides of a coin.) We can focus on the positives of that situation when the "triggering thought" tries to sneak its way back into our mind. It takes the focus off the problem and puts the focus toward a solution. Here's a very common example faced by many of my clients after their divorce.

Molly has a tough time controlling her thoughts about lifestyle changes she must make now that her divorce is final. She and Don split the assets and Molly got the house. At first, she's thrilled about it because she loves the house and all the wonderful family memories it holds for her.

The house is in a great neighborhood, and she's cultivated good friendships through the years. Fooling herself, Molly thinks she can maintain the house and continue with the same lifestyle she's been accustomed to for all these years. Eventually, reality sets in and she realizes it's clearly not possible. She must downsize, and there's no way around it.

You can imagine what's going on in Molly's mind when the self-talk starts taking over her thoughts. She thinks to herself, "I can't do this, it'll be too difficult. Am I going to be able to live in a decent neighborhood within my price range? I'm afraid and scared I'll make bad decisions because I don't know anything about selling a house."

As she experiences the self-talk, she notices there is a tremendous feeling of anxiety in the pit of her stomach. The physical feeling alerts her that she is getting "triggered".

What Can Molly Do?

Molly can start noticing her thoughts. When the negative self-talk starts, Molly pauses and takes several deep breaths. The deep breaths lift her out of self-talk and into the spiritual side of herself, which isn't trapped in thought. Then she says, "I'm having this thought. It doesn't help me move forward. I release it."

Molly acknowledges that she has the thought but doesn't get involved with it. When she doesn't get involved with it, she doesn't have to deal with the physical discomfort that thought creates. She's ahead of the "trigger" that would set her off. It doesn't mean that the present situation isn't there, but it doesn't have a hold over her mind. Since she breaks free from the hold her thoughts have over her mind, she frees herself from worrying and wasting energy. Molly can think differently about the situation by providing the appropriate space in her mind to do it.

On the other hand, if Molly feels the "triggering thought" as an uncomfortable or unsettling feeling somewhere in her body, it's her signal to change the thought at once. She changes the thought to a more empowering one.

Unfortunately, Molly has a tough time coming up with empowering thoughts or affirmations to replace negative ones. Her energy and optimism are at an all-time low. She's just transitioned through one trauma; and now she must make another major life change.

So, she works through a thought exercise I created. The purpose of it is to help her create empowering thoughts to replace the negative ones. This steers her focus towards the positives of the situation, and through repetition, it eventually helps her to look for a solution.

For this exercise I had Molly generate and write down at least ten positives of having to downsize. It coaxes Molly to start shifting her focus on the positives of the situation. (It sounds illogical and absurd but bear with me.)

Molly finds it extremely hard getting started; but once she gets going, she's on a roll and comes up with 13 positives!

As she does this, her mind becomes open and receptive instead of closed and stuck.

When her self-talk starts up again, she replaces the negative thoughts with any of the positive ones that are on her list. It helps her to focus on what's good about the situation. It's also just as important to feel gratitude for the good she presently has in her life helping her expand her thinking and welcome more abundance. It promotes a good attitude and takes the focus off what she doesn't have. Her frame of mind shifts and brings her one step closer to finding a solution instead of nursing, cursing, and rehearsing the problem. Here are three of the positives she comes up with:

1. A fresh start means a new chapter in a new house
2. Lisa, my co-worker, knows a wonderful realtor that can take me step by step through the selling process so that I feel confident doing this thing
3. Reduced home maintenance, smaller utility bills, affordable home insurance and taxes

When negative thinking about downsizing comes to mind, Molly at once focuses on the positives of the situation instead of remaining a victim of her thoughts.

Here is a link to download this exercise, https://bit.ly/3MDNW5I.

Change Our Attitude

As we begin to control more of our thinking, we foster a good attitude that is essential in changing our results. It's important to focus on our personal well-being of mind, body, and spirit. When we take care of ourselves, we reinforce the respect, worthiness, and confidence needed to change our lives for the better.

Creating effective daily habits and a routine to start the day helps us navigate our life with more success. We gain more faith and belief that we are making the best possible decisions and choices as they arise.

By creating a positive attitude towards life, it's easier to set healthy boundaries, take positive action, and cultivate healthy relationships. It allows us to navigate challenging conditions, situations, and circumstances with more dignity, control, and grace.

After divorce, many women benefit from cultivating a good attitude so that they can start each day focusing on what they can do from where they are. It creates more harmony and balance which helps them to focus on taking positive steps to move forward.

Abagail wakes up every morning with feelings of dread. Self-talk starts its incessant chatter. The aftereffects of her divorce are fresh in her mind. As a result, she doesn't take care of herself. Negative thoughts dominate her mind; and as a result, she starts the day with a bad attitude which attracts more of the same.

How Abagail Starts the Day with a Good Attitude

Abigail incorporates a daily empowerment routine in order to steer her thoughts in the direction of honoring and caring for her whole being. Self-care breeds a good attitude for staying mentally, physically, and spiritually strong as she recovers and heals from the challenges she now faces in life. Below are what she incorporates as daily habits.

- **Meditation** helps her to get in touch with her inner wisdom and power even for just a few minutes a day. (Insight Timer is a free app.)
- **Journaling** can remove mental blocks, help gain control of emotions, and help her to better understand herself.
- **Self-Care** helps her body to release sufficient energy to think clearly, get enough sleep, maintain a proper diet, and exercise.
- **Gratitude** makes her feel more optimistic about life and triggers happiness that spreads to various parts of her life. (Write three things she's grateful for.)

- **Attract a Positive Mindset** by thinking about the optimistic attitude and feelings she wants to attract today. (Daily OM app offers free daily messages of conscious awareness for mind, body, and spirit.)

Here is a link to a simple daily empowerment routine you can start with, https://adobe.ly/3SK4lcu.

By planting these strategies in my clients' minds, their inner landscape becomes a fertile ground for growth, helping to bring abundance to their outer landscape. From that foundation, it allows the coach to easily guide their client towards their goals and reap the harvest of their success.

CHAPTER 5

The Journey of Self-Knowledge: Unraveling the Essence of "Who Am I?"

By Jonathan Evans

"Knowing others is intelligence; knowing yourself is true wisdom. Mastering others is strength; mastering yourself is true power."
- Lao Tzu

The Tale of the Cheeki Rafiki: A Metaphor of Life

In the world of sailing, the story of the Cheeki Rafiki stands as a powerful illustration of the significance of the keel. The keel, acting as the backbone of the vessel, ensures that the boat remains upright, adhering to the simple yet crucial principle that the submerged weight must exceed the weight above the waterline. It's an important concept, both in the realm of sailing and as a metaphor for life. The 40-foot British yacht, manned by a skilled crew, set sail across the Atlantic Ocean in May 2014. Despite their expertise in planning and knowledge of the sea, tragedy struck unexpectedly.

Cheeki Rafiki encountered a sudden and inexplicable mishap during their homeward journey: the yacht's keel was torn away from the hull. The absence of a counterweight rendered the boat incapable of maintaining stability amidst perilous waters, resulting in the tragic loss of all individuals on board.

On the other hand, the story of another vessel, the Tao, presents a contrasting narrative to that of Cheeki Rafiki. Despite facing equally treacherous seas, Tao managed to survive, safeguarding the lives of its three French sailors. The key difference was the keel; in the case of Tao, its keel remained firmly attached. While both boats capsized, the Tao remained upside down for an astonishing five minutes before eventually righting itself. Despite the ordeal, the crew managed to stay on board for five hours before being rescued. A Hercules aircraft dropped a new life raft to them, followed by a challenging rescue operation by a cargo ship.

The keel serves as a reminder that while we may possess the skills and knowledge necessary to navigate life's challenges, it's crucial to be mindful of our identity and ensure its strength. In our lives, there lies an undeniable truth: what lies unseen in the depths of knowledge, beliefs, passion, and identity is what keeps us balanced and rights us when we keel over.

1 The Cheeki Rafiki, pictured during Antigua Sailing Week, before it ran into difficulties returning to the UK. © MailOnline

The Importance of Self-Knowledge

Abraham Maslow inspires a profound truth. *If you see yourself as a hammer, you see every problem as a nail.* Our actions are deeply rooted in our identity. Imagine this: you're heading to work and out of the blue, someone cuts you off in traffic. Now, here's where it gets interesting. If you see yourself as the epitome of calm, patience, and wisdom, you won't lose it. Nope, not even a bit. Instead, you'll whip out your secret strategies, all while sparing your horn, and presence as you tackle another day!

Here's the fascinating life hack: If you desire to change your behaviour, you can shape a new core identity for yourself. Now, I'm not suggesting that you stand in front of a mirror tonight and proclaim yourself as the smartest person in the world, expecting magic to happen. However, our beliefs shape our habits, and by consciously choosing our habits, we can mold our lives accordingly.

So, imagine that you see yourself as intelligent and consistently act upon that belief through education, reading, and surrounding yourself with intelligent individuals. Where do you envision yourself in five years? What other aspects of your identity do you wish to cultivate? Begin by defining these characteristics, and you will witness the formation of a clear plan.

Our identities are shaped in various ways. I vividly remember a home video where my grandma playfully grabbed my arm and exclaimed with a big smile, "You're nothing but a bag of bones!" I was always on the skinny side. Little did I know, I had celiac disease, which I later discovered, and which prevented proper nutrient absorption until I eliminated gluten from my diet. Although Grandma's words were innocent, they unintentionally influenced me to view myself as thin, unattractive, and insignificant. It wasn't until I acknowledged this limiting identity that I began working out and embracing a healthier, more attractive life. Just ask my wife!

There are many other events and thoughts that shape our identities. The question is: Are these identities beneficial? Even past traumatic events have proven to be enormous sources of strength and resilience for our identities. We know what we have overcome and determine that every challenge is an opportunity. It's all about reframing our stories by becoming aware of your underlying beliefs so you can make choices that will further strengthen them or shift your perspective.

Asking yourself questions like "Who am I?" "What are my goals?" and "What do I really want in life?" can open the windows to a deeper understanding of yourself. Taking the time to discover your identity is integral to unlocking your true potential and building a meaningful life. Ultimately, self-knowledge is a journey, not a destination. Uncovering who you are requires an ongoing exploration and experimentation process as we evolve over time.

No Success Without Inner Exploration

The world is filled with talented individuals, yet success can be so elusive. We often assume that education and hard work are the sole ingredients necessary for success; however, striving to reach the top is a vain exercise without deep internal exploration. Being centered and unshakable involves a foundation beyond external realities. To build a strong foundation in any pursuit requires an appreciation of self-knowledge.

In addition to becoming successful, reflecting on what success means for you is also important. Success without self-discovery can lead to feelings of emptiness, as you may find yourself enjoying the material aspects of your success but emotionally unfulfilled in other areas of life.

This double-edged sword of success holds a valuable lesson: To achieve true fulfillment, one must not only climb their way up the mountain of success but also explore what lies within.

We all have an idea of who we are, but is this version of ourselves a reflection of our true identity? This chapter will provide strategies for uncovering and understanding yourself more deeply. We'll look at self-reflection exercises, personality tests, and other techniques that will help you to gain greater insight into your thoughts, values, beliefs, and behaviours.

Understanding Self-Knowledge and Identity

Understanding ourselves is a critical aspect of achieving fulfillment and experiencing success. A firm grasp of our identity, which includes our strengths, weaknesses, passions, and values, provides a compass, guiding us towards decisions that align with our true selves. When we leverage our strengths and constructively address our weaknesses, we are more likely to succeed and find greater satisfaction in our achievements. This section explores the potent impact of self-knowledge on personal fulfillment and success and how to effectively harness this power to create a life of purpose, joy, and accomplishment.

Let's take a moment to appreciate the tragic tale of Narcissus, the Greek heartthrob[1]. This hunter was so captivating he fell in love with his reflection in a pool!

Narcissus spent the rest of his life locked in a desire with his own image, agonized by its beauty until he died. And he didn't just die – he turned into a flower! Narcissus became the very flower that now bears his name. I guess you could say he really blossomed in his self-obsession.

This ancient cautionary tale reminds us of the dangers of lacking self-awareness. If we become too absorbed in our own reflections, we might end up with a life full of empty accomplishments, unfulfilled dreams, and a warped idea of success. So, let's

avoid becoming prisoners of our own misconceptions. After all, there's a whole inner world beyond our reflections, waiting for us to explore and grow into our full potential.

The False Self

A more modern tale of pursuing the wrong interests is prominent in our success-driven society. Meet John, a Harvard-educated lawyer working at a top-tier law firm in New York. From the outside, John epitomized the model of success. He graduated at the top of his class, quickly climbed the legal ladder, and lived in a posh penthouse overlooking Manhattan. But despite his professional triumphs, John was surprisingly unfulfilled.

John had always been an artist at heart. His happiest memories were of spending hours painting by the river near his childhood home. However, dreams of becoming an artist were quickly dismissed by his parents, who were more concerned with prestige and stability. So, he hung up his paintbrushes, buried his love for art, and pursued a career in law - a path that promised societal approval and financial security.

John's days became a monotonous cycle of courtrooms and coffee breaks. He was a master in the art of successful living, but he had lost touch with his true self.

There is another tale of a Chassidic rabbi named Rabbi Zusya[2], known for his humble and timid nature. One day, as he stood before his congregation, he reflected on his own identity. When the time comes for him to face the celestial tribunal after his death, he believed they would not ask, "Zusya, why were you not Moses?" His response would be simple: "Moses was a prophet, a role I was not destined for."

Similarly, they would not question why he was not Jeremiah, the renowned writer, as he would humbly admit, "Jeremiah possessed a gift for words that I did not possess." Nor would they ask, "Why were you not Rabbi

Akiba?" For Rabbi Zusya would respond, "Rabbi Akiba was a great teacher and scholar, a path I did not follow."

Ultimately, the celestial tribunal would pose the question that truly mattered: "Zusya, why were you not Zusya?" To this, he would have no answer. This tale invites us all to reflect on our own lives and aspirations. While we strive to be exceptional leaders, parents, and partners, we must remember to be true to ourselves.

Comparing ourselves to others is a deadly trap. It robs us of our joy and the journey that only we are meant to take.

How do we discern the right path to follow? How do we live a life free of regret and of the haunting question of "why were you not?" It comes down to discovering our essence - who we are and what we will do with it.

"If you are here unfaithfully with us, you're causing terrible damage," – Rumi[3]

The 13th-century poet Rumi's wisdom is a piercing reminder of the significance of being faithful to our true selves. Living a life that is not congruent with our inner desires and passions inflicts damage not only to ourselves but also to the collective human experience. When we suppress our true identities and conform to societal expectations or pressures, we essentially withhold our unique contributions, talents, and perspectives from the world. We are all here for a purpose; we all have unique gifts to offer. When we choose authenticity over conformity, we invariably cultivate a richer, more vibrant world.

As we each embrace our unique paths and live our truth, we collectively paint the world with a vibrant mosaic of diverse experiences, further enriching human culture and evolution.

Have you ever met anyone in a mid-life crisis? I've been there! I had a fancy office, bespoke suits cramming my closet, lots of degrees and certificates on the wall, a beautiful website, a sportscar and a LinkedIn profile with thousands of followers. Then it hit me - Who are you trying to impress? What is all this for? In a moment of reflection and clarity, I realized, "You're not fully loved until you are truly known." I was creating an impression of success and working hard for my respect and value - but all those things weren't really who I was. You see, without self-knowledge, we cannot love ourselves and have others love us for who we truly are.

When we were young, we created strategies to protect ourselves, and they served their purpose and shaped us into who we have become today. I always followed the trends to protect my social status whether it was wearing acid-washed jeans, listening to Vanilla Ice on my discman and memorizing sketches from Saturday Night Live to impress my peers. However, just like a mask, these identities must be stripped away to live authentically with ourselves and others. We rob ourselves of true love when we live out of false identities. Our rewards and relationships are based on a fabrication.

In her groundbreaking work, *The Gifts of Imperfection*, Brené Brown brings to light the profound role of vulnerability and courage in cultivating self-knowledge and authentic relationships. Brown propounds that vulnerability often misconceived as a weakness, is indeed a measure of courage. It's the birthplace of innovation, creativity, and change. Embracing vulnerability implies acknowledging our imperfections and fears, thereby unravelling the core of our identity. As we confront our vulnerabilities with courage, we start to disentangle our authentic selves from the façade we've built to protect us from judgment and criticism. This self-revelation deepens our self-knowledge and enhances our relationships with others. By showing up authentically and fearlessly expressing our true selves, we invite others to do the same, fostering genuine connections founded on mutual acceptance and understanding. Brown's insight underscores the significance of vulnerability and courage in our journey towards self-discovery, personal fulfilment, and meaningful relationships. Truly, the only real offering you can give is your own authentic self.

Unleashing your authentic self is the key to living a fulfilling life, one where love and acceptance are not bound by pretenses but are rooted in your true identity. Personal fulfillment and the opportunity to offer your individual gifts to the world await on this self-discovery journey. The question remains, "How do I discover who I truly am?" We will turn to Jung to answer that.

Jungian Theory and Self-Knowledge

Carl Jung, the Swiss psychiatrist and psychoanalyst, introduced several archetypes that he believed were universal across cultures and within the collective unconscious[5]. The following are some of the most commonly recognized Jungian archetypes:

1. **The Self**: This unifying archetype signifies the integration of an individual's conscious and unconscious mind. It's the archetype that represents the individual's realized sense of self.

2. **The Shadow**: This archetype embodies the personal unconscious, representing parts of ourselves that we might reject or repress, such as anger, envy, or selfishness. Embracing and understanding the Shadow can lead to personal growth.

3. **The Anima/Animus**: According to Jung, each person carries within them aspects of the opposite gender. For males, this is the Anima (the feminine inner personality), and for females this is the Animus (the

masculine inner personality). These archetypes help us understand our relationships and interactions with the opposite sex.

4. **The Persona:** This archetype represents the image we present to the world, often acting as a mask that protects the Ego from negative images. It can be seen as the social version of ourselves that we present to others.

5. **The Hero:** The Hero embodies courage, strength, and resilience. This archetype is often seen confronting fears and embarking on a journey.

6. **The Mother:** The Mother archetype is not only about literal motherhood. It represents nurturing, caring, fertility, and life-giving aspects in general.

7. **The Father:** As an archetype, the Father represents authority, protection, and discipline. It symbolizes a guiding force or an authority figure.

Understanding these archetypes can provide valuable insights into our behaviours, motivations, and interpersonal relationships. They guide our journey towards self-discovery, helping us understand who we are and why we behave in certain ways.

The Collective Unconscious, with its archetypes, is like a universal databank of human experiences, a reservoir of our shared heritage. It holds our ancestors' wisdom, experiences, and understandings of the world. This collective memory influences our individual behaviour patterns and life experiences.

Understanding and integrating these archetypal themes within our personal narrative allows us to access the wisdom of the ages. We can uncover our deepest fears, motivations, and potential, allowing us to realize our authentic self. As we become more conscious of these unconscious influences, we start to live more authentically, harmonizing our personal experiences with our inherited collective wisdom. This journey of alignment with the Collective Unconscious is a transformative process leading to self-discovery and personal evolution.

Popular Personality Tests

Personality tests are over a $500 million industry growing at 10% to 15% per year. Organizations and individuals eagerly embrace these tests each year in their pursuit of self-awareness. As an executive coach, I utilize several assessments to facilitate effective team communication, enabling them to understand one another's values, beliefs, preferences, and personality types. The questionnaires help people become more aware of themselves and incorporate this knowledge in their careers and relationships.

Here is a list of some of the most widely used personality tests, along with brief descriptions of their effectiveness and origin:

1. **The Birkman Method:** The Birkman Method, developed by Dr. Roger Birkman in the 1950s, is a self-assessment tool that provides insights into a person's interests, behaviours, and motivational needs. It's highly effective in personal development, career coaching, leadership development, and human resource management. However, it's less commonly used in clinical or research settings.

2. **Myers-Briggs Type Indicator (MBTI):** The MBTI was developed in the early 20th century by Isabel Briggs Myers and her mother, Katharine Cook Briggs, and was based on Carl Jung's theory of psychological types. Using four dichotomies: extraversion-introversion, sensing-intuition, thinking-feeling, and judging-perceiving, it categorizes people into 16 personality types. While widely popular in business and personal development contexts, it has faced criticism for its lack of empirical evidence and reliability.

3. **DISC Assessment:** The psychologist William Moulton Marston's work was the basis of this assessment developed in the 1920s. The DISC model categorizes behaviours into four types: Dominance, Influence,

Steadiness, and Conscientiousness. It's an effective tool for understanding interpersonal communication styles and team dynamics, but it's not intended to predict or evaluate psychological states or mental health.

4. **Strength Deployment Inventory (SDI):** The SDI, created by psychologist Elias H. Porter in the 1970s, focuses on understanding people's motivational value systems and how they respond to different situations, especially during conflict. The SDI's strength lies in its application within team dynamics and conflict management.

5. **Gallup Strengths Finder:** Now known as Clifton Strengths, this assessment was developed by Don Clifton, the father of Strengths-Based Psychology, in collaboration with Gallup. It measures natural talents across 34 themes, helping individuals identify their top strengths. This positive psychology approach has been widely applied in personal development, team building, and leadership development. However, its ability to predict job performance or satisfaction is subject to ongoing research and debate.

6. **Enneagram:** This assessment, derived from the Greek words 'ennea' (nine) and 'gramma' (point), was popularized in the 1970s by the Bolivian psychiatrist Claudio Naranjo. The test identifies nine personality types that represent their own individual

perspective and archetype that reflects how people feel, think, and act in connection to others, the world, and themselves. Proponents of the Enneagram argue that its value lies more in its descriptive and diagnostic capabilities, which foster deep self-understanding and personal transformation.

Personality tests have a strange allure indeed; it's like a peek into a crystal ball, but for your own traits and quirks. After all, who doesn't enjoy learning more about themselves and then broadcasting the results? "I'm an ENFP!" we declare, as if it's a newly discovered Hogwarts house. "Oh, you're a 'Commander'? Charming, I'm more of a 'Debater' myself!" we toss around at cocktail parties, and suddenly, we're a walking, talking Myers-Briggs Type Indicator.

Emotional Intelligence

Did you know that 80% of people who are limited in their careers are not stuck because of intelligence or skill but emotional intelligence? Daniel Goleman is famous for popularizing emotional intelligence[6].

Emotional Intelligence is defined by Goleman as, "the ability to recognize, understand, and manage our own emotions and the emotions of others." It's an important tool for effective communication, collaboration, relationship management, and leadership. By understanding our own emotional patterns, we can better recognize the subtle cues given by people around us, which allows us to build better relationships and interpret situations quickly and accurately.

These psychological tools allow us to gain insight into our emotional makeup and ultimately create a more self-aware and balanced life. When we come to understand ourselves, we can build better relationships, work effectively in teams, manage our emotions properly and become better leaders. We can finally realize our true potential and live authentically with acceptance of who we are. Fundamentally, studying our personality and improving self-awareness and self-management leads to better relationships and career success.

The Hero's Journey and Self-Knowledge

Once we have explored what sort of character we are, we must determine what journey we are on. Joseph Campbell's concept of the Hero's Journey offers a transformative blueprint for self-discovery and personal growth[7]. It's not merely a narrative structure we find in myths and stories from around the world, but it's also a metaphor for our personal journey toward self-knowledge. This universal narrative echoes our life's adventure, marked by trials, tribulations, revelations, and, ultimately, transformation.

As we embark on this journey, we encounter challenges that push us beyond our comfort zones, requiring us to tap into our inner strength and resilience, akin to the hero within each of us. By understanding and embracing the stages of the Hero's Journey, we not only gain insights into the narratives that shape our lives but also unlock our potential, allowing us to lead fulfilling lives true to our authentic selves. This journey inward is indeed the most heroic journey of all, for it requires the courage to confront our shadows, embrace our inner light, and emerge as the heroes of our own stories.

Stages of the Hero's Journey

Joseph Campbell's Hero's Journey, or the Monomyth, is typically divided into three main sections: Departure, Initiation, and Return, each comprised of multiple stages.

Departure

1. **The Call to Adventure:** This is the beginning of the journey where we feel the urge to venture into the unknown. This represents the moment in our life where we realize there's more to learn about our identity and purpose.
2. **Refusal of the Call:** Often, fear or reluctance hold us back from embarking on this journey of self-discovery. We may resist change a refuse to step out of what we deem as comfortable.

3. **The Supernatural Aid:** This symbolizes our mentors, guides, or personal revelations that provide the necessary courage or insight to take the first step. This could be a significant book, a friend, or a life-changing event.

Initiation

4. **The Crossing of the First Threshold:** This is the point of no return when we fully commit to our journey of self-discovery and leave behind the familiar.

5. **The Belly of the Whale:** This represents the stage of isolation and introspection, where we confront our deepest fears and insecurities.

6. **The Road of Trials:** Here, we encounter various challenges and obstacles that test our resolve, each one offering opportunities for growth and self-understanding.

7. **Meeting With the Goddess / The Ultimate Boon:** This stage involves realizing a profound truth or achieving a significant goal. A moment of clarity brings a deeper understanding of our purpose and identity.

Return

8. **The Refusal of the Return / The Magic Flight:** After achieving our boon, we may hesitate to return due to satisfaction with our current state or fear of losing what we've gained.

9. **The Crossing of the Return Threshold:** We return to the familiar world but with new wisdom and insights about our identity. This is a moment of integration, where our newfound knowledge becomes a part of our daily life.

10. **Master of Two Worlds / Freedom to Live:** We've now reconciled our outer world with our inner self. We're in harmony with ourselves, fully aware of our identity, and live authentically.

Recognizing these stages in our life can provide a roadmap to our personal journey of self-discovery. By understanding where you are on this journey, you can better appreciate your struggles, celebrate your victories, and uncover the narrative that shapes your identity.

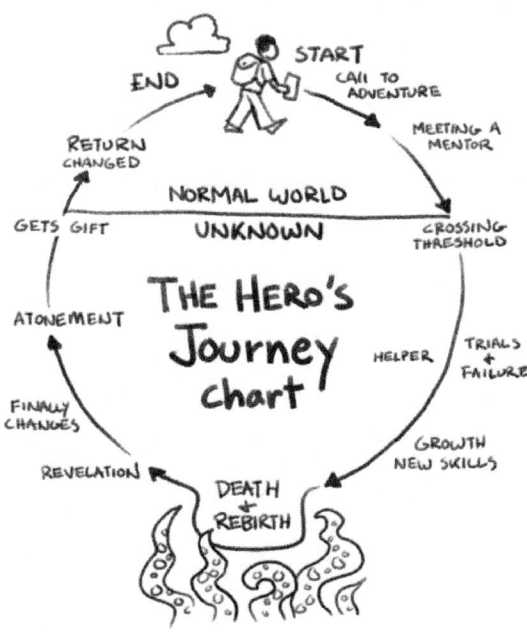

2 Image - Kanbanazie (https://www.arcstudiopro.com/blog/the-heros-journey)

The Hero's journey is a cycle of embarking on an adventure of growth, death and rebirth.

Expanding the Self-Knowledge Model Through Experimentation and Reflection

Consider George Foreman, the two-time World Heavyweight Boxing Champion. Foreman's life is an allegory for our journey of self-discovery and personal growth. Foreman enjoyed a meteoric rise to fame in his youth, becoming the World Heavyweight Champion. However, like the hero in our journey, he was soon ushered into a period of trials and tribulations. In 1974 Muhammad Ali challenged Foreman to a championship fight in the Democratic Republic of the Congo called the Rumble in the Jungle. At that time most bets were on Foreman. Ali, the former heavyweight champion, was seven years older and, most believed, past his prime.

Foreman had been undefeated and planned on maintaining his title. "I took the fight because I could knock him out in two rounds," he said. "I thought, '$5 million for two rounds? Wow!' " However, Ali used George's confidence against him with his infamous "rope a dope" strategy and knocked Foreman out. The once formidable champion found himself in the Belly of the Whale, isolated and confronting his deepest fears and insecurities.

But Foreman did not remain in this abyss. Instead, he found his Supernatural Aid in the form of faith, becoming a pastor and embarking on the path towards self-discovery and introspection. This transformative journey led him to confront his past mistakes, accept responsibility, and consciously commit to change.

Foreman's Road of Trials didn't stop there. He faced numerous financial and legal obstacles, but each one offered an opportunity for growth and self-understanding. He eventually regained his heavyweight championship in his forties, exemplifying this profound truth, a resilience in the face of adversity to form a deeper sense of self and to live authentically in the world.

Foreman integrated his new wisdom with his past experiences in the final stages of his journey. He reconciled his past's rough edges with his newfound sense of self, using his experiences to inspire the world, capitalize on his success, and live authentically for others.

As we delve deeper into the realm of self-knowledge, it's essential to recognize that our understanding of ourselves is not static but an ongoing process shaped by our experiences and interactions. It's like one big experiment that molds us into the quirky, unique individuals that we are. By deliberately placing ourselves in diverse situations, we uncover layers of our personality and character that remain hidden in the comfort of familiarity. This active engagement with the world around us, coupled with thoughtful reflection, paves the way to solidify our self-knowledge and, in turn, our identity.

So, if you want to uncover your true potential, face all of these challenges head on. There are many challenges to embrace in your journey of self-discovery. Here are how these challenges can strengthen you on your journey of self-discovery.

Physical Challenges

Physical challenges such as engaging in a new sport or pushing our endurance limits teach us determination, resilience, and the importance of maintaining our health. Each sweat drop enriches our perception of our capabilities and boosts our self-confidence.

Mental Challenges

Mental challenges, such as learning a new language or solving complex problems, stimulate intellectual growth and foster a mindset of continuous learning. They sharpen our cognitive abilities and provide a sense of accomplishment, enhancing our self-worth.

Social Challenges

Social challenges, like public speaking or leadership roles, test our interpersonal skills and empathy. They expose us to diverse perspectives, helping us understand

and embrace differences, thus nurturing our emotional intelligence.

Spiritual Challenges

Spiritual challenges, involving practices such as fasting, meditation or retreats, offer a pathway to introspection and higher consciousness. They inspire us to discover the purpose of our existence and seek a deeper connection to life beyond the physical realm.

Creative Challenges

Creative challenges, like writing a poem, painting, or learning to play a musical instrument, provide an outlet for self-expression. They allow us to tap into our innate creativity, unleashing our unique perspective and artistic flair.

Environment Challenges

Interactions with our natural environment, such as hiking, camping, or even gardening, instill a sense of tranquillity and foster a deep appreciation for the interconnectedness of all life forms.

By embracing these diverse challenges, we allow ourselves to grow, evolve, and gain a multifaceted understanding of our identity. Each challenge is an experiment that contributes to our self-knowledge and shapes our perception of who we are.

Conclusion

Life, in essence, is an exciting voyage of self-discovery, a journey toward understanding the core question — "Who am I?" Just like a boat's keel keeps it upright and stable, self-knowledge is our keel, providing stability and direction amidst the turbulent waves of life. It offers us a clearer perception of our personality, values, emotions, motivations, and even untapped potential.

However, our understanding of self is not as straightforward as it seems. It's a complex interplay between the 'false self', the persona we present to the world, and our 'true self,' the person we are at our core. Popular personality tests offer us insightful snapshots of our psychological makeup, but they are not the final word on our identity. To truly understand ourselves, we must write our own Hero's Journey. We must face and overcome our trials, confront and embrace our weaknesses, and integrate our newfound wisdom into our experience. Finally, the journey to self-knowledge is a constant process of experimentation and reflection. It's a wild roller coaster ride, full of crazy twists and turns, and at the end of it, we come out stronger, wiser, and more self-aware.

So, as we conclude Chapter 5, remember that the journey to self-knowledge is not a sprint but a marathon. It's a lifelong commitment to exploring the depths of our being, to understanding and accepting ourselves, warts and all. We must embrace this journey with humour, compassion, and an open mind. After all, as they say, the journey itself is more important than the destination. Happy discovering!

CHAPTER 6:

Life's Values and Principles

By Victoria Ivchenko

"The meaning of life is to find your gift. The purpose of life is to give it away."
- Pablo Picasso

Many of us can appreciate the empowering feeling that comes from having our value recognized by others. I believe this to be one of life's most impactful experiences. It would then follow, as we contemplate the driving forces of our existence, that the most meaningful pursuits are those by which we can share our ideas, creations or services, to positively affect, influence, and inspire those around us. But life can be full of many different types of rewarding experiences.

So how does someone define true fulfillment and determine which paths are the ones that can lead us there? Such questions have puzzled even the most introspective minds throughout millennia. The search for answers gradually resulted in the formation of various studies, sciences, and schools of thought, which continue to specialize in helping examine and resolve many of the intricacies that plague the human psyche. The rise in demand for new insights from such fields of study was no coincidence. Our postmodern world continues to witness an ongoing increase in the number of people who suffer from various types of emotional and mental afflictions.[89]

This trend is partially a result of our biological template's inability to keep up with our rapidly changing society[10]. Fortunately, with the guidance and services offered by professionals in coaching, counseling and therapeutic fields, individuals are able to improve their emotional and mental competencies and take charge of their lives with greater efficiency, responsibility, and strength of character[11]. This chapter will offer a few viewpoints for consideration, as you contemplate how the values of happiness, purpose, and fulfillment apply to your own personal journey. It will also explore the importance of understanding and utilizing our inherent resources to achieve the goals we set for ourselves, as we navigate the changing terrains of our lives.

On Happiness

The pursuit of happiness, once considered an abstract notion, received a historic rebranding when it was included in America's Declaration of Independence by its Founding Fathers, who codified happiness into the list of mankind's "unalienable rights"[12]. With time, the revised concept of happiness settled into the collective consciousness of North American culture and became seen as an integral part of quality of life.[13] Paradoxically, exercising the right to happiness has proven to be a struggle for many individuals, despite improvements in other aspects of their living standards[14]. But much like perfectionism, it's important to remember that happiness is a moving target[15]. Although it remains as one of the prominent objectives that many people strive for in life, happiness can be interpreted in different ways. World-renowned spiritual teacher and author of The Power of Now, Eckhart Tolle defines happiness as "...a heightened sense of aliveness attained through physical pleasure, or a more secure and complete sense of self attained through some form of psychological gratification"[16]. This definition serves as an important reminder that, if we are not careful, happiness can easily be confused with pleasure. This can lead to addiction, which can end up taking many victims down a dangerous rabbit hole and in a direction quite different from the paths leading to genuine fulfillment.

In his book Sapiens, which explores human history, psychology, and anthropology, Noah Yuval Harari states, "...happiness consists of seeing one's life in its entirety as meaningful and worthwhile". The same sentiment was also shared by Viktor Frankl,[17] a neurologist, psychiatrist and founder of logotherapy. Frankl published his autobiography Man's Search for Meaning following his liberation from the Holocaust concentration camps at the end of the Second World War. Frankl believed that life's meaning is accrued from the quality of attention and level of responsibility people dedicate to handling each life situation, as well as in the way that an individual endures times of inevitable suffering, which are often an inherent part of the experience of life.[18]

Frankl also adds that we come to find our true purpose through our interaction with the external world, as opposed to searching for it exclusively inside our own psyche[19].

In other words, by cultivating a thorough intrapersonal (of the self)[20] understanding, each individual improves the quality of their interpersonal (social)[21] connections, thereby increasing the level of potential positive impact one can have in their relationship with both themselves and the external world.

Ultimately, each person's pursuit of self-discovery should begin with a deep understanding of their inner character. The importance we place on our core values, - be it freedom, happiness, success, love, or any pursuit of a similar essence, - determines the dedication with which we strive to achieve our goals and achieve self-actualization – that is, embodying the full scope of our potentialities[22]. This is no simple feat, but with the right kinds of emotional and psychological tools, and the ability to use them, we stand a better chance at succeeding in our quest for self-fulfillment.

On the Importance of Our Emotional Toolkit

Any successful venture, be it for the purpose of business, travel, or personal development, relies on diligent planning, preparation and securing the required tools and resources to effectively handle anticipated obstacles. Our life's journey is no different. As humans, if we neglect to cultivate the right kinds of inner skills, we run the risk of stunting our emotional, psychological and spiritual growth. In addition, we limit the opportunities available to us that can help us achieve our true potential. The way in which we handle our emotions plays a fundamental role in determining the quality of our experience in life[23]. Some examples of skills that facilitate better emotional management include emotional intelligence and mindfulness of our attitudes, beliefs and perceptions. These skills have a tremendous influence on our behaviors, reactions and the choices we end up making.[24][25]

In his book *Emotional Intelligence: Why It Can Matter More Than IQ*, psychologist and science journalist Daniel Goleman reminds us that our rationality is governed by our emotions.[26] This is due to the fact that our emotional brain predates its rational counterpart by millions of years.[27] Goleman links the definition of emotional intelligence to self-awareness, as both require dedicating attention to the changes of one's feelings and inner states.[28] Given that responsible decision-making is a byproduct of a controlled mental state,[29] a dysregulated emotional domain can result in some adverse consequences including, "...a spectrum of risks, from depression [..] to eating disorders and drug abuse".[30] One of the main methodologies of therapeutic and coaching professions involves restructuring obstructive cognitive patterns,[31] so as to allow for a greater depth of reflection, efficiency and responsibility in the client's decision-making. Part of this process involves working on improving the quality of our outlook and attitudes. In addition to increasing the risk of various categories of disease,[32] pessimistic attitudes limit us by restricting the scope of opportunities and our ability to recognize them. An optimistic disposition, on the other hand, is not only beneficial for our health, but also helps improve our psychophysiological coherence, - a term from Penney Peirce's book, Frequency: The Power of Personal Vibration. Peirce describes psychophysiological coherence as an efficient and harmonious relationship between the body's systems, resulting from sustained positive emotions.[33] A good attitude can also be useful in improving our problem-solving skills, by helping identify available opportunities and solutions, and/or creating new and improved alternatives where none may appear to exist.[34] Attitudes have also been proven to play a key role in fostering "luck" in a person's life, by inspiring confidence to allow for the optimization of opportunities.[35]

Another way to optimize our experience of life is to discover and develop our aptitudes. In his book *The Element: How Finding Your Passion Changes Everything*, Ken Robinson presents several inspiring testimonies of accomplished individuals who found both fulfillment and success through the dedicated pursuit of their talents and passions. Robinson stresses the importance of recognizing that all of us possess a wide range of capacities, including "imagination, intelligence, feeling, intuition, spirituality and physical and sensory awareness".[36] The book also expresses the author's concern with the limited scope through which intelligence is measured by the education system and various standardized testing methods.[37] The author warns that failing to understand one's true intellectual abilities can prevent people from discovering their Element.[38]

Success, on the other hand, stems from embracing the diversity of our intelligence through the dynamic use of our brain and the different ways in which we experience the world.[39] Accordingly, another vital component of discovering our Element lies in the power of creativity and its relationship with imagination and intelligence.[40] Readers are informed about some misconceptions regarding creativity and reminded that anyone can develop the ability to be creative. Creativity is not restricted to certain fields. Since creativity is not an exclusively inherent skill, it can be developed at any point in life[41], thereby allowing us to be creative in any venture.

When engaging in activities that we feel truly passionate about, we may notice a physiological fluidity in the way we operate, as well as a sense of feeling energized and in alignment with the process.[42] Robinson refers to this state as "the flow", which can be defined as the fusion of our energies and abilities with opportunities during the pursuit of a goal, and the intrinsic gratification that is experienced from this process as a result.[43] Some of the benefits of the flow state include an increase in energy levels and a sense of effortlessness in the accomplishment of required tasks.[44] Robinson also examines some of the perceived barriers that can prevent individuals from pursuing their passions. Drawing reference from bestselling author Susan Jeffers' book Feel the Fear and Do It Anyway, Robinson identifies fear as one of the primary obstacles to finding one's Element[45] and provides examples of various fears that can hold people back from exploring the full scope of their potential. These include the fear of not being good enough, fear of disapproval, fear of failure and the unknown, among a few others.[46]

In overcoming some of the apprehensions that we may encounter on the road to self-discovery, we must keep in mind that there is no deadline to be missed when it comes to soul-enriching pursuits. In fact, some capabilities can even improve over time,[47] and "different capacities express themselves in stronger ways at different times in our lives".[48] We can facilitate these types of expressions by taking care of our physical and mental health, being diligent with our diet, exercise and attitudes, as well as through emotional fine-tuning practices, such as meditation.[49] In conclusion, it's by cultivatating a deep understanding of the full scope of our capabilities and dedicating ourselves to developing and applying them in ways that are aligned with our goals and values, that we improve our chances of achieving a truly fulfilling and meaningful experience of life.

Now that I've covered (to the best of my ability) the information promised in the introduction of this chapter, I would like to take a moment and speak personally about my own pathway to finding fulfillment. During my studies at the University of Toronto, my program and course selection criteria were based exclusively on my personal interest in the subjects of sociology and world religions. I loved learning about the various human dynamics that interconnect and shape our cultures and societies, which factors and patterns influence our behavior, and what inspires and motivates us as individuals and as a collective. I admit, after graduating and upon entering the workforce, I spent quite a few years second-guessing my decision of not getting a degree in a more practical field, such as social work or teaching. Although I always enjoyed working with people, I never felt that my knowledge and potential were being sufficiently utilized through the services I was providing or within the capacity of the job title I carried. When I began my practice as a life coach, everything in my essence felt stimulated by the learning and experience I gained in this field. I found myself spending majority of my free time immersed in supplementary reading material, eagerly feeding my curiosity on all things having to do with mental, emotional, and spiritual hygiene. It did not take long to notice substantial improvements in my own feeling, thinking, and behavior patterns. After all, as life coaches, we need to be at least a couple of steps ahead in terms of the "work" we guide our clients to do in their own lives. Achieving a sense of empowerment in my own life, through the various changes and practices I adopted during my personal learning journey, has allowed me to better resonate with my clients and provide guidance that's sourced from first-hand experience, and not just textbook knowledge.

If your takeaway from this chapter were to be narrowed down to one word, it should be "eudaimonia".

"Eudaimonia" is defined simply as "the pursuit of that which is worthwhile in life".[50] The origin of this term can be traced back to the Golden Age of ancient Greek philosophy, where the great minds of Aristotle, Socrates and Plato attempted to investigate the science of happiness.[51] Although we don't quite have it down to a science yet, we all deserve to pursue those things in life that ignite our curiosities and fuel our passions for learning, helping, and creating. For it is by honoring our commitment to pursuits in which we find meaning, that we can discover and fulfill our individual purpose. And, for those of us lucky enough, inspire others to do the same.

CHAPTER 7

Journaling - Dialogue with the Self and Harnessing the Power of Reflective Writing

By Carla Jaclyn Harding

Introduction

Journaling, at its core, is a dialogue with the self. Through the art of reflective writing, you initiate conversations with the most authentic aspects of who you are. It's a sacred space where the conscious and subconscious merge, thoughts and emotions find their voice, and the heart whispers its wisdom. Within these pages, we shall unravel the various paths of journaling, all of which can lead to self-discovery. They will help you to realize that it's not just about the pen and paper, but about bridging the gap between your outer reality and your inner self. This sacred bridging can then lead to self-awareness, self-acceptance, and, most importantly, self-love. For, it's by journaling that you will finally hear the deepest part of the self through the noise of the external world.

Becoming Aware of Thought and Belief Patterns

Journaling is a powerful tool in the realm of self-exploration and self-discovery. It creates a sacred space where you can engage in profound conversations with your inner self. By putting your thoughts and feelings on paper, you gain a clearer understanding of the internal dialogue that shapes your self-perception. This process is about more than just writing; it's a process of deep introspection and self-discovery.

As you embark on your journaling journey, you begin to peel back the layers of your thoughts and belief patterns. This unveiling is a significant step towards transformation. You start to recognize the self-limiting beliefs that may have held you back, and the empowering thoughts that can propel you forward. The act of journaling serves as a mirror reflecting the complexities of your inner world. It allows you to confront your fears, acknowledge your strengths, and ultimately, choose a path of self-empowerment. It motivates you to take inspired action or flip the script of your limiting beliefs to create the life you've always dreamed about.

Journaling allows you to recognize any fears that are holding you back from taking risks. For example, one may have the fear of success. So, in your journal, ask yourself; "What does success mean to me?", "Why do I fear success?", and "How can I turn those fears into a catalyst for personal growth, empowerment, and transformation in my journey toward embracing a successful and fulfilling life?".

Having the fear of success is one of the most common reasons why we don't pursue our dreams and aspirations. Those fears program the subconscious mind to believe that we don't deserve to be successful and that we're inherently bound to failure. However, challenging this belief through journaling involves recognizing that the fear of success is often rooted in self-doubt and limiting beliefs.

What are the top three limiting beliefs that can hinder you from your path to success?

1. **Fear of Failure:** The belief that failure is a definitive and negative outcome can prevent individuals from taking risks or pursuing their goals. Overcoming this belief involves reframing failure as a learning experience and an essential part of the journey toward success.

2. **Imposter Syndrome:** Many people struggle with feeling like they don't deserve their achievements, attributing their success to luck rather than their abilities. Overcoming imposter syndrome requires recognizing one's competence and understanding that success is often a result of hard work and capability.

3. **Scarcity Mindset:** Believing that there is a limited amount of success, opportunities, or resources to go around can lead to a mindset of competition and comparison. Shifting to an abundance mindset involves understanding that success is not finite and that there are ample opportunities for everyone.

By reframing these fears, acknowledging our worthiness of success, and embracing the possibilities that come with achieving our dreams, we can reprogram our subconscious mind. Success then becomes not only attainable but a natural outcome of our efforts. It's a journey of self-discovery and empowerment, where we replace the fear of success with the confidence to manifest our aspirations and live a fulfilling life aligned with our true potential.

You must also examine what taking a risk looks like. While taking risks looks different to everyone, here are a few examples of ways you start taking risks.

1. **Set Clear Goals and Prioritize Them:**
   - Define your short and long-term goals. Understanding what you want to achieve provides a roadmap for taking purposeful risks.
   - Prioritize your goals to focus on what truly matters. This clarity helps in identifying which risks align with your objectives.
2. **Step Outside Your Comfort Zone:**

- Identify areas where you feel comfortable and challenge yourself to go beyond those boundaries.
- Start with small, manageable risks and gradually increase the level of challenge. This gradual approach builds confidence and resilience.

3. **Embrace a Growth Mindset:**
   - View challenges and failures as opportunities for learning and growth rather than as setbacks.
   - Cultivate a mindset that values the process of learning and improvement. This perspective makes it easier to take risks, knowing that even if things don't go as planned, there's value in the experience.

Remember, calculated risks are strategic and involve careful consideration of potential outcomes. Taking risks doesn't mean being reckless; it means being willing to step into the unknown to pursue opportunities for growth and success.

In this sacred dialogue with yourself, you become aware of just how much influence your thoughts have on your self-esteem and overall well-being. This heightened self-awareness is the first step towards embracing your true self and fostering self-love. Through journaling, you not only observe your thought processes but also learn to reframe them, replacing self-doubt with self-compassion. This transformative journey is an opportunity to shed the weight of the past and to begin constructing a future filled with confidence, self-acceptance, and the realization of your deepest dreams.

Awareness of Self-Talk

Begin by becoming acutely aware of your inner dialogue. The first step is to notice what triggers you have and write those down. Are these conversations happening when you're alone, in social situations, or during certain emotions as a result of being triggered by someone or something? When you become aware of your triggers, you can then acknowledge and accept the thoughts, feelings, and emotions that are coming to the surface.

The second step is to ask ourselves, "Why am I being triggered?" Is it because of a past trauma, or is it because your beliefs don't align with those around you? For example, the belief system of not being good enough or feeling like you don't deserve to follow your dreams because you've been conditioned to live up to the expectations of societal standards. Asking yourself "why?" is essential in peeling back the layers of those triggers so that you can release the pain, anger, and resentment of the past.

Journaling allows you the space to have that dialogue with yourself, to realize that you are, in fact, good enough, and that you do deserve to be happy.

Creating a Safe Place for Journaling

Creating a safe space for journaling is an essential and transformative component of the journey of self-discovery. The transformation arises not only from the space itself but also from the intentional act of establishing an environment that encourages openness, reflection, and personal growth. Just as a gardener nurtures the soil to allow seeds to grow, your journaling space becomes the fertile ground where your inner thoughts and emotions can flourish. In this space, there is no judgment or fear, only acceptance and self-love. It's a haven where you can be your most authentic self, explore the recesses of your soul, and confront the shadows of your past. This safety net, woven from your intentions and the physical or mental space you create, provides the nurturing environment necessary for your authentic essence to bloom and for you to ultimately build the life you've always dreamed of, rooted in self-awareness and empowerment.

To embark on a journey of self-discovery through journaling, first find a serene and comfortable space where you can be alone to connect with your inner self. Seek out a place that resonates with your soul, whether it's a cozy corner within the sanctuary of your home or the embrace of nature's beauty. The choice of location is significant because it sets the stage for the profound connection, you're about to establish with your inner being. In this tranquil setting, you can escape the distractions of the external world and create a sacred space to commune with your true self.

What are some examples of what a safe space can look like for you?

1. Cozy Reading Nook:

Set up a comfortable and quiet reading nook in your home. Use soft cushions, blankets, and perhaps a dim lamp to create a warm and inviting space. This dedicated spot can become your personal sanctuary for reflective journaling.

2. Nature Retreat:

Find a peaceful spot in nature, such as a quiet park, a serene garden, or a secluded beach. The natural surroundings can provide a calming backdrop for introspective writing, allowing you to connect with your thoughts in a tranquil environment.

3. Personal Retreat Space:

Designate a specific area in your home as a retreat space for self-reflection. Decorate it with items that hold personal significance, such as meaningful artwork, inspirational quotes, or symbols that resonate with your spiritual journey. This space serves as a refuge for contemplative journaling.

Remember, the key is to choose a location that resonates with you and makes you feel secure and at ease. Creating a safe place for journaling enhances the quality of your introspective dialogue and supports your journey toward self-discovery and empowerment.

It's in this space where the spiritual essence of your being starts to unveil itself. You'll find that, over time, you become more attuned to your inner voice and the wisdom it holds. This process of self-discovery is a profound and ongoing journey, one that leads you towards a deeper connection with your authentic self and, ultimately, a more loving and accepting relationship with yourself. In this sacred space, you can embark on a path of transformation, building the life you've always dreamed of, guided by the light of your inner spirit.

Setting the Intention

When you embark on your journaling practice, it's important to approach it as a sacred container for your inner exploration and healing. What is it that you feel led to write about? Do you need to let go of pain and resentment from past experiences? Do you want to tune into what truly makes you happy so that you can do the things that you've always wanted to do? Do you need to let go of the fears and self-doubt that are preventing you from making your dreams a reality? There's no limit to what you can and will write about.

Your journal becomes more than just pages filled with words; it's a sanctuary for your deepest thoughts and feelings. It's a space where you can be completely authentic, without judgment, and be vulnerable with yourself. This sacred container is where you can lay bare the intricacies of your soul and truly connect with the essence of who you are.

As you open your journal and put pen to paper, remember that you are stepping into a realm of self-exploration where honesty is your most trusted companion. Here, you are free to express your fears, dreams, regrets, and hopes. It's a place where the weight of past pain can be released, and self-love can flourish. By holding an intention, you create an environment where you can witness your growth and healing unfold on the pages before you.

Setting an intention is a powerful practice that involves consciously focusing your thoughts and energy on a specific goal or desired outcome. Here are three steps to guide you through the process:

1. **Reflect on Your Values and Desires:**
   - Take some quiet time to reflect on what matters most to you. Consider your values, passions, and goals for the long-term.
   - Consider what you want to invite into your life or achieve. This could be related to personal growth,

relationships, career, health, or any other area of your life.

- Be specific about your intention. Instead of a broad goal, such as "be happy," consider a more concrete and actionable statement like "cultivate joy in daily activities."

2. **Phrase Your Intention Positively and Affirmatively:**

- Frame your intention in a positive and affirmative language. Instead of focusing on what you want to avoid, concentrate on what you want to attract.
- Use words that evoke a sense of empowerment and possibility. For instance, if your intention is related to health, phrase it as "I am cultivating a healthy and vibrant body" rather than "I don't want to be sick."
- Make it personal and align it with your values. The intention should resonate with you on a deep level.

3. **Create a Ritual for Setting Your Intention:**

- Choose a consistent time and place for setting your intention. This could be a part of your morning routine, during meditation, or before bedtime.
- Develop a ritual to accompany the process. This could involve writing your intention down, saying it aloud, or visualizing it in your mind. Some people find it helpful to create a vision board that represents their intention.

- As you set your intention, focus on it with a sense of belief and positivity. Feel the emotions associated with achieving your goal.

Remember, setting an intention is not a one-time event but an ongoing practice. You may choose to revisit and revise your intention as your circumstances and growth evolve. Consistency and belief in the process are key elements in the effectiveness of setting intentions.

Your journal becomes a mirror reflecting the depths of your being. It's where you can converse with your inner self, forging a profound and transformative connection. Journaling is a form of self-love and acceptance, providing a platform to acknowledge your true feelings and thoughts. Through this practice, you empower yourself to navigate the winding paths of your spirit, ultimately building the life you've always dreamed of, rooted in self-awareness and self-compassion.

Centering Yourself

In your journey of self-discovery and self-love, taking a moment to center yourself is a powerful practice. It all begins with a few deep breaths. As you inhale deeply, you draw in the energy of the present moment, letting go of the chaos of the outside world. Exhaling slowly, you release any tension and concerns. With each breath, you become more attuned to the rhythm of your own being. This simple act of conscious breathing helps you reach the intersection of your inner and outer worlds.

With your eyes closed, you enter a realm where your inner self takes center stage. In this sacred space, acknowledge any emotions or thoughts that surface. Honor them without judgment, whether they are a gentle whisper or a tumultuous wave. This space is where authenticity is cherished, and vulnerability is your strength. As you connect with these inner currents, you begin to recognize the depth and complexity of your spirit. Each emotion and thought you acknowledge is a piece of your unique tapestry, an integral part of the beautiful mosaic that makes you who you are.

This practice of breath and introspection paves the way for self-discovery and self-acceptance. In these quiet moments, you lay the foundation for a more profound love and understanding of yourself. By giving space to your inner world, you can start to unravel the mysteries of your being. As you build this connection, you empower yourself to shape the life you've always dreamed of, rooted in self-awareness, self-compassion, and a deep appreciation for your spiritual essence.

As a result, intention building emerges as a natural extension. With each intentional inspired action, you consciously shape a vision for the life you aspire to lead. As you align your intentions with the love, understanding, and self-discovery cultivated through journaling and introspection, you embark on a purposeful journey toward manifesting the life you've always dreamed of and becoming the person you are destined to be.

No Editing Required

When you put pen to paper in your journal, let your thoughts and feelings flow freely, unencumbered by judgment or self-censorship. This sacred act of writing is your unfiltered connection to the depths of your soul. It's like a sacred canvas where you're invited to paint the raw, unfiltered truth of your existence, allowing the essence of your being to unfold without any embellishments. Embracing this space enables a profound connection with your authentic self and fosters a journey of self-discovery in its purest form or facet of your existence; even the parts you might have previously deemed imperfect or flawed. As the ink flows, so does the river of your self-discovery and healing.

As you journal, also consider the profound connection to your spiritual essence that this practice offers. Recognize that you are a divine being on a journey of self-discovery, an explorer of your soul. This awareness can be a source of tremendous strength and motivation. It reminds you that, within you, there's a wellspring of wisdom and an innate connection to something greater than yourself. It's a gentle but powerful affirmation of your intrinsic worth and significance. Your journal becomes the scroll on which you inscribe the chapters of your self-discovery journey, allowing you to chart your path with self-compassion and self-empowerment, weaving a narrative of profound self-love.

Journaling with a Grateful Mindset

Upon concluding your journaling session, take a moment to express gratitude for this precious time of self-reflection. Gratitude is the key that unlocks the door to a more profound connection with your authenticity. It's a gesture of acknowledgment for the journey you've just undertaken within yourself.

Embracing gratitude in journaling not only enriches the exploration of inner thoughts and emotions but also becomes a guiding light on the journey toward self-discovery and empowerment.

What are some ways you can practice having a gratitude mindset while journaling on your dialogue with the self?

1. **Gratitude for Self-Discovery:** Acknowledge moments of self-discovery and personal growth. Express gratitude for the lessons learned and insights gained through introspection. This practice is important as it encourages continual self-awareness and spiritual evolution.

2. **Appreciation for Inner Strength:** Reflect on instances where you exhibited resilience, courage, or inner strength. Show gratitude for the capacity within yourself to overcome challenges. This is crucial as it reinforces a positive self-image and fosters confidence in facing future uncertainties.

3. **Thankfulness for Present Moments:** Express gratitude for the current moment and the opportunity for self-reflection. Recognize the value of being present with your thoughts and emotions. This practice is significant in cultivating mindfulness and deepening the connection to your spiritual essence.

Why is expressing gratitude in a self-dialogue journal important? Knowing the "why" behind the importance of holding gratitude while journaling provides a profound understanding of how this practice serves as a transformative tool for nurturing self-awareness, fostering a positive mindset, and cultivating a deeper connection to oneself.

1. **Promotes Self-Love:** Gratitude for self-discovery and inner strength contributes to a sense of self-love and acceptance. It encourages embracing both strengths and areas for growth with kindness.

2. **Cultivates Mindfulness:** Thankfulness for the present moment promotes mindfulness. Being aware of

your thoughts and feelings in the now enhances spiritual consciousness and connection.

3. **Fosters Positivity:** Gratitude in self-dialogue shifts the focus from self-criticism to self-appreciation. This positive outlook contributes to a healthier inner dialogue and overall well-being.

As you bask in this moment of reflection and gratitude, you validate the importance of self-discovery and self-love and create a positive ripple effect that can extend to every aspect of your life.

Gratitude is not just an afterthought; it's a vital component on your journey of self. It's an affirmation that you are thankful for the opportunity to explore your inner landscape, to nurture self-acceptance and self-love, and to be in touch with your divine essence. This act of thankfulness magnifies the power of your journey of self-discovery and lays the foundation for a more harmonious, fulfilled life. So, as you close your journal, be sure to embrace gratitude as a daily ritual that not only empowers your spirit but also keeps you aligned with the path of self-discovery and self-empowerment you've chosen to tread.

4 Types of Journaling Exercises

Now that we have explored what reflective writing is and why it's important, let's explore the different types of journaling exercises you can implement to help you become more aware of your inner dialogue, and flip the script.

Letter to Your Inner Self

Write a heartfelt letter to your inner self, the part of you that needs love and healing. Share your thoughts, fears, and dreams in this letter. Be compassionate and forgiving in your words, as if you are offering comfort to a dear friend. Writing letters to yourself to acknowledge your hard work can be a beautifully transformative practice. The process can help you find pride in your persistence and can profoundly impact your well-being. This process of self-affirmation and self-recognition creates a positive feedback loop, reinforcing your commitment to self-improvement. It's a powerful way to cultivate self-love and reinforce your spiritual essence.

In these letters, you're not only acknowledging your accomplishments but also celebrating the journey itself. By doing so, you honor your inner strength and resilience, allowing you to connect more deeply with your true self. This practice can help you stay motivated and remind you of your capacity to overcome any challenges that may arise.

Ultimately, writing letters to yourself as an expression of pride is a manifestation of self-compassion, which is an essential component of any personal development journey. It fosters self-acceptance, self-appreciation, and self-empowerment.

Affirmation Writing

Create positive affirmations that resonate with your self-discovery journey. Write them down not only in your journal, but on sticky notes as well and place them where you'll see them regularly. They can be placed on mirrors, walls, or taped to your computer. You can even have the same affirmation written down and placed throughout your home or apartment.

Repeating these affirmations can help you cultivate self-love and acceptance. I've also found that setting aside a page or two in my journal and writing my affirmation 50 times is extremely therapeutic. What affirmation you use should be unique to you and be in alignment with the goals and intentions you have set when beginning to flip the script on your thought and language patterns.

Write down a list of things telling yourself what it is that you love about yourself. For example, "I love my_____". This can be done once a week or once a month. This journaling exercise is extremely therapeutic and healing in allowing you to step outside of the boundaries of external validation and acceptance.

Gratitude Journal

Write down what you are grateful for in your life. This practice can help you focus on the positive aspects of your journey and foster a sense of contentment and self-acceptance. I recommend listing 5 things each day that you're grateful for. But take it a step further; ask why you are grateful for the things and people in your life. Ask why you are grateful that you've achieved that goal you've been working towards. When you know the why behind it, it deepens the feeling of gratitude even further.

Dialogue with Your Higher Self

Write a conversation between your current self and your higher self. Ask questions, seek guidance, and receive answers through your writing. This can be a profound way to connect with your inner wisdom and find self-compassion. Your questions could look something similar to:

You: "Today I'm trigged/grateful for...."

Higher Self: "Why are you feeling this way?"

You: "I'm feeling this way because.......

Higher Self: "How can I become less triggered and not react in a way that is not in my best interest?"

From there, let your thoughts flow freely onto the page. It really is beautiful and amazing what comes through when we tune out everything going on around us, sit in silence, and just be with our thoughts, feelings, and emotions and with our pen and journal.

How Journaling Can Be Used to Release Past Wounds and Improve Self Awareness

Exploring Past Wounds

Start by delving into your past experiences that have caused pain or left emotional scars. Recall the situations, people, and emotions associated with these wounds. You may relive some of those feelings as you write, which is why reflective journaling is so impactful. It provides a space for us to become more aware of our emotional triggers so that we can reflect upon ways to let go of the past and no longer become triggered by the actions and words of others.

Release and Let Go

Putting your pain into words is cathartic. As you see the words form on the pages, you're releasing the emotional energy tied to these past wounds. Imagine that you're transferring the pain onto the pages, allowing it to exist outside of yourself. You'll start to notice how much lighter you feel by releasing the energy of those emotions. Once this is done, rip it up and throw it in the trash. The act of tearing paper can be a surprisingly cathartic and spiritual experience. It represents shedding or releasing something, similar to the process of letting go of emotional baggage in one's life. This simple act can symbolize the therapeutic journey of releasing past pain and embracing self-love; aligning with the core principles of flipping the script on your inner dialogue. There is no need to go back to re-read it and rehash it repeatedly. You let the pain stay in the past where it belongs.

Forgiveness and Compassion

As you write, you might find it easier to forgive those who have caused you harm or forgive yourself for past mistakes. This is a deeply spiritual aspect of the process, as forgiveness is seen as a pathway to healing and inner peace. This is why I find letter writing so impactful. You can also write letters of forgiveness to others who may have caused you harm.

Maintaining a Consistent Journaling Practice

Maintaining a consistent journaling practice is a beautiful way to embark on a journey of self-discovery. Journaling doesn't require rigid outlines or bullet points; instead, it's an opportunity to create a sacred space for your inner thoughts and emotions to flow freely.

To start, find a quiet and serene place, preferably in the morning or before bedtime, where you can connect with your inner self. This connection to the divine within is essential for having a deep and profound dialogue with the self.

Be consistent in your journaling. When you are consistent with your writing, the more in tune you will become with your thoughts and feelings. Consistently journaling at a set time each day fosters a commitment to transforming your inner dialogue.

Maintaining consistency in your journaling practice empowers you to explore your inner world to discover who you are at the core. Ask questions like "What are my core beliefs?" or "What brings me inner peace and joy?" These inquiries will help you unravel the layers of your authenticity, bringing clarity and insight. Remember, there's no right or wrong way to approach this; it's a personal journey of exploration.

Reflect on milestones of personal growth and resilience. Celebrate your achievements and acknowledge your challenges with compassion. Journaling acts as a mirror, revealing your inner beauty and potential. Through this process, you'll learn to fully embrace and accept yourself, fostering a profound sense of self-love that extends to every aspect of your life. Your journal becomes a sanctuary for the evolution of your self-discovery.

While journaling, it's essential to remain neutral and non-judgmental. Your journal should be a safe space to express your thoughts and feelings without criticism. As you pour your heart onto the pages, you'll discover the wisdom and guidance that exists within you.

Ultimately, maintaining a consistent journaling practice is a powerful tool for uncovering your true self, and deepening self-love on your transformative journey.

Carla Jaclyn Harding
Empowerment Coach and Author
Email: selfempowermentwithcarla@gmail.com
Website: https://www.selfempowermentcoach-ingwithcarla.com

CHAPTER 8

Meditation and Mindfulness: The Practice of Presence

Exploring Consciousness as a Tool for Self-Understanding
By Selbia Leon

Introduction

The art of coaching involves guiding individuals to achieve their goals. Becoming a professional Life Coach has been a process; it has not been easy. As a counselor, I have always been confident that knowing your inner self allows you to connect with your divine consciousness. It was a battle at the beginning of my work as a professional Counselor and then becoming a Certified Life Coach.

In the process of learning and practicing new techniques and ideas to help my clients achieve their goals, overcome their challenges, and reach their full potential, I discovered that I should pay attention to the present moment to be able to practice effective communication during my sessions. This journey begins by exploring consciousness as a tool for self-understanding and channeling these different approaches proactively during my sessions with my clients.

The following key aspects contributed immensely to my current practice as a Life Coach. Those keys are effective communication, building relationships, empathy and emotional intelligence.

Effective Communication

First, practicing being present provided me with the skills to have effective communication, the ability to listen actively, ask powerful life changing questions, and provide my client with constructive and motivating feedback.

By paying attention to the space and time around me I became more aware of the present moment; noticing that I was alive, breathing, and part of the most beautiful reality, which I created without giving myself credit. I was now noticing that something extraordinary was happening, and I enjoyed that moment of complete presence

I was entering into the fantastic practice of seeing my smile, paying attention to my breathing, perceiving my senses, and observing my body movements. Practicing living in the present moment brings clarity to the mind and a divine connection to self-knowledge and self-consciousness; this is the art of mindfulness.

Building Relationships

Practicing being present and willing to listen created the perfect moment to establish trust and rapport with my clients. I began to identify the barriers I had created during my client sessions and began to create a supportive and safe environment where they feel comfortable sharing their thoughts, feelings, and challenges.

I understood my position as a Life Coach was to be something other than an advisor. I was there to give them the tools to expand their wisdom and innate knowledge. These exposures provided me with the opportunity to expand my knowledge and experiences with new tools that I could use to benefit my clients with a more comprehensive integrated approach.

Empathy and Emotional Intelligence

Meditation and mindfulness create the perfect environment to expand life coaching services in a holistic way. Empathy allowed me to be attuned to my client's needs and comprehend that my clients are in the driver's seat instead of myself, the coach. It provided the proper conditions for this collaborative approach during sessions. The coach is there to support clients' goals and help them develop their own style; to explore and discover their own interventions and encourage them to research their solutions.

Incorporating my counseling knowledge with the Life Coach techniques provided me with the tools to help clients set clear, specific, and achievable goals for their discovered interests and aspirations.

Then the question is, how can you integrate meditation and mindfulness into your practice?

Meditation and mindfulness provide you with the tools to practice mindfulness and to explore awareness as a tool for self-understanding.

In conjunction with exploring consciousness as a tool for self-understanding, mindfulness and meditation has been a critical part of my professional practices and daily life. When your client is fully engaged in the present moment, they will have the ability to connect and focus their attention on leaving behind past issues and avoiding anxieties surrounding their future, without judgment or distraction.

This comprehensive approach to the practice of mindfulness and meditation methods has become part of my personal life and professional services. Practicing being present by embracing the now cultivates awareness of one's thoughts, emotions, and sensations in the present moment. By engaging in the now, one can be more attuned to what is happening in their surroundings; there is an excellent connection to one's own experiences and an awareness of one's inner states.

Various techniques are available to expand your practices, such as meditation, breathing exercises, mindfulness practices, Tai Chi, and journaling. To maintain mindfulness in my personal and professional life, I learned that I must go within myself daily to make the connection between the conscious mind and body of my higher self.

Training my attention through mindfulness has helped me enjoy the present moment and focus on my wellbeing. Developing knowledge and self-mastery by practicing presence and self-awareness has a positive effect in all areas of a person's life.

One of the most complex parts of having awareness and practicing mindfulness is the ability to create a skillful mental habit, to remain committed and continue to explore consciousness as a tool for self-understanding.

Beneficial Elements for Your Mindfulness Practice

There are three key elements that I use during my journey when practicing mindfulness that will be beneficial to you in your practice. These elements are:

- Self-awareness, which can be internal self-awareness and external self-awareness
- Self-Regulation
- Motivation

Self-Awareness

Self-awareness, or being aware of your present moment, feelings, and conscious mind, is critical. Self-awareness means having the ability to understand and recognize oneself by paying attention to one's thoughts, feelings, behaviors, and identity.

Self-awareness can be discovered by asking self-discovering questions such as, what is my intention related to this process? What do I want to discover? Asking self-discovering questions can be beneficial as it promotes inner self exploration and reflection on one's own thoughts, feelings, and actions.

There are diverse ways to promote self-awareness and self-discovery within your practice, but I suggest two types of self-awareness that have been key to my professional practices. The first type is **internal self-awareness**, which involves the person's understanding of their own emotions, values, and personal beliefs.

This type of mindfulness improves attention and concentration and reduces self-judgment. When you can guide your clients to identify their strengths and weaknesses, they can have a clear understanding of how their actions impact others and themselves.

The second type is **external self-awareness**. This type starts to develop when you can accurately perceive how others view you. External self-awareness involves understanding how your behaviors impact others and how you see yourself from an outside perspective. This development of consciousness helps to have better relationships and improves empathy.

Exercising mindfulness is an ongoing process that can lead to a deeper understanding of oneself and a more fulfilling life. Self-awareness does not imply achieving a perfect knowledge of oneself but continuously attempting to know and comprehend yourself better.

Self-Regulation

Self-regulation is an ability that is gained through the insight of your life experiences. This Self-regulation ability connects to our thoughts, emotions, behaviors, and desires, and we use them as resources to connect with our personal goals. When you can observe and maneuver your actions and reactions, your internal consciousness induces you to achieve your desired outcomes.

Motivation

Motivation is the inner call to growth, or the drive and determination to pursue one's goals. Motivation helps us to maintain a clear intention and to focus on the completion of the desired destination without losing our visions. This motivation might take us out of our comfort zone; this is part of the process. With these key elements you can knock down your personal barrier and enter the magical world of mindfulness!

Mindfulness

Mindfulness relates to paying attention and having a purpose in the present moment without judgment. This level of awareness helps us to regulate our emotions. Self-mastery comes with training your attention, developing self-knowledge and practicing mental habits that reveal your inner truth. Living in the now, in the present moment, helps you to let go of the connection to those things that don't give you a clear sense of purpose in life.

Going within during mindfulness meditation internalizes those existential questions, such as what is your purpose in life? Are you fulfilling that purpose? And who are you serving with your purpose? Being aware of your environment, reflecting on yourself as a conscious being, and understanding your needs provide the stage to transform your reality and perceive and know your inner self more in-depth.

Exploring your life purpose with consciousness will bring attention to how you perceive things around you. You will have the understanding that you can transform your environment. You can change the settings within you! You might have resistance to change or transforming your current environment, but this is part of the process of self-awareness.

The practice of being present and being in the moment can help you celebrate your reality in the middle of chaos. When you connect with your inner self, breathing, and consciousness, you directly connect with your truth. This way, you can have deeper connections in your relationships and enjoy a more meaningful life.

During the process of mindfulness, you may learn to embrace the moments of total silence. At first that connection may be scary, but if you close your eyes and pay attention to the present moment that silence will fill your heart. Feel your presence, pay attention to the current moment, to the space you are holding, embrace the energy you are feeling, and see how the noise becomes a stranger in your world of silence.

The best thing that can happen to your human existence is the unification of your consciousness and self-love, uncovering the most significant expression of your own truth. Stop being afraid of who you truly are and become comfortable connecting with your inner consciousness. Through self-reflection, we are consciousness connected without labels, opinions, or judgment. You are unique, and you have the power to create. That is your divine call!

Pay attention to your heartbeat and breathing and set your intentions to create the life you want. Let silence show you the beauty of the sound! Silence can teach you the absolute expression of your human divinity and wholeness. In silence, there are no measures, no time-lines, only the now exists!

So, mindfulness practice is the art of living consciously!

Eternally in love with myself!

Selbia Leon,
Certified Spiritual and Life Coach

CHAPTER 9

Creative Visualization

By Ghazaleh Emambakhsh

"Close your eyes and visualize having what you already want - and the feeling of having it already."
– Rhonda Byrne

Introduction

16 years ago, I came across *The Secret* by Rhonda Byrne (Byrne 2006). My mom had purchased it but hadn't started reading it yet; when I picked it up and saw *The Secret*, my curiosity peaked immediately - what kind of secrets could this book hold? Soon thereafter I became riveted and soon realized it was about visualization as an effective means for reaching the dream of living our ideal lifestyles.

My curiosity soon led to research. With each question that came my way, more case studies surfaced regarding the power of visualization, such as the case of Chris Hoy from Scotland. Hoy was one of the key cyclists in the early 2000s and, using visualization before every race, would picture perfect technique. After reading that case study as well as another concerning Chris Hoy's visualization journey, my own visualization journey began.

After discovering visualization's potential through The Secret and real examples like Olympian Chris Hoy's training tactics, I eagerly dove deeper into research such as Dr. Guang Yue's (Yue, G. & Cole, K.J. (1992) which revealed neuroplasticity - the brain's ability to create new neural pathways through repetition. Yue's brain scans demonstrated that mental visualization could activate regions matching brain activity for physical action, explaining imagination's influence over outcomes. Creative visualization intrigued me - how could simply picturing goals manifest tangible results as the research has proven? My quest to unlock this skill compelled me deeply to study visualization's inner functioning myself.

Sixteen years later, having cracked codes strengthening mind-matter connections daily, here I am writing to you all about how visualization has transformed my mindset and life from ordinary to extraordinary. What an exhilarating journey it has been! At first, I tried visualizing small things such as traffic lights...

Eager to stretch my visualization muscles, I started small - picturing all green lights on my daily commute. Concentrating deeply, I focused intently on picturing each green light in sequence throughout my route. At first, matching external signals with my internal visualization was haphazard. But repeatedly running this mental movie of smooth flows did not go to waste - gradually, more traffic signals aligned to my mind's direction just as envisioned! Soon I was visualizing prospering in new dance moves. By mentally mastering each step, my body gracefully followed suit! Creative visualization had awakened stunning cognition-to-reality crossover abilities within me through consistent picturing aligned to purpose.

So why creative visualization, you might ask? I realized some visualization techniques are like casual conversations. Others like creative visualization, which involves deeper meaningful connections, feel like heart-to-heart conversations. This shows commitment to one's wishes, like carefully working dough between your palms to shape a creation. No wonder why so many people love working their hands in dough.

Understanding Creative Visualization

What exactly is creative visualization?

Creative visualization is the practice of conjuring vivid mental imagery to imagine desired outcomes as being realized. Instead of passive daydreaming, creative visualization requires focused concentration and active engagement of one's mind to picture specific scenarios with greater detail than daydreaming can offer. By repeating these mental rehearsals over and over, one can train their brain to bring these possibilities to fruition.

Research has established that visualizing stimulates similar parts of the brain as an actual sensory experience. Brain imaging studies by Kosslyn, Ganis, and Thompson (2001) indicated this by showing that physical motion visualization triggers the motor areas and picturing piano playing activates the coordinated finger movement regions. Overall, vivid images are processed just like real perceptions or actions.

Multisensory images have the most dramatic results because creative visualization engages all five senses to form vivid, lifelike mental scenes. Dedicated practice concentrates on these multilayered sensory memories, priming our subconscious towards manifesting desired outcomes.

Over time creative visualization also helps establish neural pathways necessary to align thoughts, emotions, and actions to desired results. It provides the mental blueprint that helps bring those outcomes into reality.

Now that we understand what creative visualization is and its ability to recreate real experiences within our brains, let us review key techniques for applying it effectively. Guided imagery, affirmations, meditation, and creative writing are effective methods of creative visualization. They immerse us fully into visualizing desired outcomes and can strengthen focus, mindfulness, and inner creativity.

Creative Visualization Techniques

Guided Imagery

At first, when I heard of guided imagery, I thought it involved simply daydreaming what you wanted - how wrong could I have been! Guided imagery takes daydreams one step further by turning visions into reality.

Guided imagery involves taking timeouts in your day to visualize your goals in vivid detail, with all their sights, sounds, and feelings as real experiences. Sometimes adding in ambient sounds or music can add extra layers!

Imagine yourself practicing your free throw skills: Envision each shot sliding with ease into the net. Knees bent, elbows aligned, the ball softly rolling off your fingertips as it cuts straight through the net with an audible "Swoosh!" Hear the crowd go wild when the basketball's path to the net becomes clear.

Your subconscious learns by watching vivid, realistic mental movies. Doing this often enough will convince the subconscious that this new reality exists resulting in an unconscious alignment! Your mind can accomplish much more when directed clearly towards a bright goal!

Make the most of every moment you spend daydreaming - take charge and direct it towards where you want it to go! Utilize guided imagery techniques to write, practice, and rehearse a movie of your goals coming to fruition. You may be amazed at what unfolds when immersing yourself regularly into goals and visions! Lights, camera...imagine!

Affirmations

Many underestimate the power of affirmations, believing they're nothing but meaningless positive mantras. I can assure you otherwise: affirmations can act like rocket fuel when combined with creative visualization!

Affirmations are the practice of taking the visualizations and dreams you have floating in your mind and speaking to them aloud as though they already exist. For instance, if you imagine yourself performing on stage one day, instead of thinking "I wish I were a great performer" instead say with conviction, "I am an enthusiastic performer with impressive stage presence who engages audiences!"

Passionate affirmations program your brain to support what you desire. For instance, telling yourself you want to become a sought-after performer initiates the vision, then creating momentum along the way as your vision comes alive through actions, thoughts, and feelings of accomplishment.

So, start declaring one or two powerful statements that define your goals every day aloud with feeling. See what unfolds when your imagination gets an audible boost!

Creative Writing

Believe it or not, putting pen to paper can help make your biggest dreams come true! Expressing your goals and visions through writing is a surprisingly powerful visualization technique. All you need is an open mind and creativity. Describe your ideal outcomes in detail. Let the words spill out unfiltered. Add vivid sights, textures, and feelings. Let your true aspirations flow from mind to page.

Then indulge your imagination fully in storytelling! Bring your visions alive through poetry, journaling, and fiction. Giving narrative shape to your mental images makes them feel more real. Writing brings clarity to your desires and releases self-doubt. Capturing your dreams in Technicolor engages your mind deeply. This creative process strengthens your visualization over time.

Start small by setting aside 10 minutes each morning to write out your visions, goals, and ideal scenarios.

Meditation

Meditation and creative visualization make for an impressive combination! Silencing your racing thoughts will allow your mental visions to emerge more vibrantly than ever.

Discover a quiet space to sit comfortably. Take slow, deep breaths focusing on each inhalation and exhalation. If distracting thoughts enter your mind briefly acknowledge them before gently shifting back towards breathing.

As your body relaxes and your mind settles into calm stillness, begin visualizing. Imagine yourself fulfilling your goals, vividly. See yourself confidently presenting an address before an attentive audience with calm assurance. Hear and see your voice projecting outward, feel your steady assured movements. These images should guide your visualization process and lead you toward fulfilling them with vivid imaginings of success.

Eliminating distractions enables deeper focus on mental imagery as it unfolds. Even consistent 5-10 minute visualization sessions during morning and nightly meditation markedly boost abilities over time.

Creative Visualization Tips

1. Set Clear Intentions:

Be specific in setting your intentions; don't just vaguely visualize success, be specific! Establishing specific goals provides focus and direction while including details like dates, amounts, and locations can bring these intentions alive. "Find my soul mate," may be difficult to envision; therefore, an alternative goal might be, "meet a loving, fun partner who enjoys travel and hiking by next summer".

Try to visualize meeting this ideal partner among your friends and family as you hike together. Picture this new relationship from all perspectives - the more exact and specific your imagination gets the better it works!

2. Consistent Visualization:

Frequent practice of visualization is much more effective. Set aside dedicated time each day, most find first thing in the morning or right before bed to be most beneficial. Even 5-10 minutes of consistent visualization practice can rewire your mind's pathways over time while also cementing the ritual as a predictable daily habit. Make a visualization ritual at that same place and time each day! (Edited)

Schedule this meeting with yourself, and do not cancel it! Regularly visualizing strengthens neural pathways supporting your intentions over time. Daily practice also offers invaluable feedback that shows when adjustments need to be made in approach.

3. Troubleshoot Obstacles:

Doubt, distractions, and impatience can obstruct visualization. Notice them without judgment. Doubts can often arise from unhelpful beliefs that inhibit positivity, so label any distracting thoughts as unwelcome interruptions before gently shifting focus back onto visualization.

Impatience often stems from having unrealistic expectations about timing. Change occurs gradually; trust that consistent visualizing sets unseen forces into motion in the universe's perfect timing. Commit yourself daily instead of demanding immediate results.

4. Expansion

Once you become adept at applying creative visualization in one area, use it in others, such as health, career, finances, relationships, or personal growth. Practice those until your mind quickly starts activating *creative visualization mode*. Switch the topic every session or perform brief visualizations across many topics at the same time.

The Power of Visualization: Inspiring Case Studies

Creative Visualization can be an engaging field. What convinced me the most was witnessing people use these techniques to enhance their lives through the continued practice of visualization. Allow me to present some inspiring case studies:

Maria was an experienced marathon runner who focused each evening on crossing the finish line within 3 hours and 30 minutes on race day. She was successful and she even broke her personal best by over five minutes! It worked exactly as imagined (Alison & Bennie 2020).

James was an ambitious entrepreneur. Driven by his visions of giving presentations with ease and raising investor funding effortlessly, new opportunities began presenting themselves. Within months he gained two major clients as well as capital (Taylor & Wilson 2005).

Natalie, an aspiring surgeon-in-training, struggled with anxiety and errors during operations. By visualizing herself as being calm, and focused, and leading each surgical step flawlessly, Natalie was able to provide significant relief to her anxious feelings. Within one year Natalie rose through the ranks at her hospital, becoming one of its premier surgeons (Arora et al. 2011).

These real-world examples confirm my belief that ordinary people can access extraordinary mental capabilities through intentional visualization. Just as weightlifters train muscles consistently over time, mindful training of your mind reaps dividends; use this evidence as motivation on your visualization journey.

Conclusion

As I conclude this story of creative visualization and its transformational impact on me, I hope my experience inspires others to harness their imagination through guided imagery, vision boards, affirmations, and meditation techniques for better mental well-being. Creative visualization has helped improve my clarity, reduce stress levels, and align my goals more accurately over time. Using guided imagery, vision boards, affirmations and meditation consistently manifested my desires. If this interests you, I encourage you to give these methods a try for yourself; start small by visualizing modest goals becoming a reality each week while working diligently toward fulfilling them. Your latent creative potential will unlock even greater amounts of mental creativity for sure!

Continue to gain knowledge on how visualization affects your subconscious and shapes reality. Commit to a daily visualization practice that uses daydreams of achievable objectives and activates an inner force to help build the life you imagine for yourself. Visualization provides this skill.

Imagine, believe, and manifest! Your imagination holds infinite potential that needs unlocking. Start practicing visualization today. Just set aside 10 minutes each morning in a calm space to relax your mind, visualize goals fulfilled, and track changes over time. Unleash the power of creative visualization for manifesting what's in your imagination into the tangible!

Visualization creates reality! Your imagined future awaits, manifested reality!

Byrne, R. (2006). The secret. Beyond Words Publishing.

Stewart, C., & Hoy, C. (2004). The Flying Scotsman: The Graeme Obree and Chris Hoy Story. Birlinn.

Yue, G. & Cole, K.J. (1992). Strength increases from the motor program: Comparison of training with maximal voluntary and imagined muscle contractions. Journal of Neurophysiology, 67(5), 1114-1123.

Kosslyn, S.M., Ganis, G., & Thompson, W.L. (2001). Neural foundations of imagery. Nature Reviews Neuroscience, 2, 635-642.

Alison, M., & Bennie, J. (2020). Strategies for improving marathon performance through visualization: Case study. Journal of Applied Sport Psychology, 32(4), 392-399.

Taylor, J., & Wilson, G. S. (2005). Applying sport psychology: Four perspectives. Fitness Information Technology.

Arora, S., Aggarwal, R., Moran, A., Sirimanna, P., Crochet, P., Darzi, A., ... & Grantcharov, T. (2011). Mental practice enhances surgical technical skills: a randomized controlled study. Annals of surgery, 253(2), 265-270.

CHAPTER 10

Movement to Unlock a Better You

By Tuomo Vauhkonen

To move is to be human.
-Rich Roll

Movement is a fundamental part of a thriving life for us as human beings. If we observe nature and our Ecosystem, nothing is static. Everything, including plants, animals, the air we breathe, and the water we drink is in continuous dynamic movement. The cycles of growth and decay follow each other as life keeps evolving through this on-going natural dance.

To not move is to resist nature's most natural flow. The more effective choice is to throw yourself into this flow and to influence its direction, because movement is and always will be an elementary part of life, nature, and how we exist in the world.

Yet the current lifestyle of many people is in direct opposition with nature's flow. We live sedentary lifestyles where most people walk less than 4000 steps a day. This has now become an independent risk factor for cardiovascular disease as a long-term health concern. (Source).

Obesity, heart disease, and cancer are at an all-time high in the Western World. Yes, we may live longer than before, *but are we living better or just suffering more?* This is a haunting thought that will hopefully make you reconsider your lifestyle choices. With advancements in medicine and healthcare we've managed to prolong our lifespan, but that may not be the case with health span.

I believe that movement is one of the most important keys when it comes to unlocking health, a thriving lifestyle, and a better future for you. And the best aspect of this solution is it doesn't require complicated treatment protocols.

The exact opposite, that is solutions being simple, can be more truthful and effective. In addition, we get to learn and connect with ourselves at a deeper level. Hidden corners of our internal landscape can be revealed to us through Movement, because when the physical body moves, so does our emotional and mental energy.

Unstuck Yourself

Movement literally releases our internal blocks and stuckness. Just think of how energized and calm you feel after a great run, dance class, or hike up in the mountains. I have seen people burst into tears on the massage table as their muscles released and moved energy through their nervous system.

When we move ourselves, we literally move our internal energy throughout our body as well. This can, and often does, release repressed emotions and reveal thoughts and insights that were once unattainable.

This is how movement allows space for self-discovery. The outside-in approach through movement is a powerful tool for personal growth and development.

There is a term closely related to Movement, which is **Proprioception.** In a nutshell it means *how our body senses the world around us and finds stability and balance in it.* These aspects of movement play key roles in how effectively we can move through the environment we inhabit.

Physical movement is liberating. It has value for everyone as Movement allows a free expression of ourselves. There is a myriad movement-based activities that movers have adapted free of structures and limitations. We now express ourselves freely through activities like dancing, trail running, free flow yoga, calisthenics, and surfing, to name just a few.

Most competitive sports have also morphed into these non-competitive forms that offer a different approach. By making one of these movement practices easier to connect with we can express ourselves better due to the less competitive nature of that activity.

Most simply said, Movement = Freedom

To me, movement has always been a source of internal inspection, a safe haven from my internal demons, and something that has and will always be a fundamental part of who I am.

Movement and Flow

Flow is a state where we feel our best and perform our best.
-Mihaly Csikszentmihalyi

Movement is the marriage between challenge and skill, where all focus and concentration hone in on the present moment. All the worries of the future or the past are put aside for a moment, and we're fully engaged. We move freely in complete harmony and understanding with the activity we are engaged in.

It can be a jazz musician playing together with his band, a surfer sharing the waves with the ocean, a painter who creates beautiful images for hours without pause, or a public speaker who loses a sense of time on stage.

One of my many experiences with the flow state was when I gave a TEDx Speech, "Why Lifestyle Matters More Than Happiness" in Tahiti. I completely lost a sense of time as my full concentration came to the present moment. Luckily, the speech was well rehearsed, and I didn't pass the strict TED eighteen-minute time limit. Even today I can only remember the opening lines and the outro of my stage performance, and everything in between is a blur. It was a short yet deep experience of flow state. I was fully present, performing at full capacity and potential. These are *Peak Life Experiences* (PLE's for short), which I would like to create more of.

The common denominator in these states of Flow is the presence of Movement, whether it's emotional, mental, or physical. Surfing and writing are two of my favorite flow activities, one engages the body and the latter engages the mind.

So how does flow and movement help with self-discovery? When we feel our best and push the boundaries of what we thought wasn't possible, we learn and grow. We find out what makes us feel truly alive and stay in the present moment. To connect with flow means to be at our very best without any masks, hesitation or feelings of inadequacy.

And if movement results in freedom, then freedom leads to flow. And when in flow everything about reality is more vibrant and alive.

7 Principles and Habits to Add Movement into your Life.

Design your Environment for Movement

The popularity and knowledge surrounding the power of Epigenetics is beginning to spread into discussions around health and wellness. *Epi* (above) means that there is an external effect on our genetic expression, and this effect comes in large part from our environment (as well as our thoughts and emotions).

This means that the physical environments we inhabit have an effect on our health down to our DNA. If you live in congested city jungles surrounded by high rise buildings as opposed to the beach or the mountains, it's probably clear which environment is better for natural movement.

One way to add movement into your life is to inhabit or visit spaces where movement is naturally inviting and exciting.

Set Goals Based on Daily Movement.

Our mind is a goal seeking machine. It's continuously seeking targets and outcomes. So, we might as well feed our brains what it's asking for. The popular 10.000 steps a day idea isn't originally based on science or research, but it turns out that it's a beneficial marker for health.

I personally set movement-based goals in weekly intervals which allows substantial buffer time to miss a day here and there. Since *life happens,* it's good to have guidelines that allow us more flexibility, but also opportunity for results.

Instead of being too strict, especially in the beginning when establishing a movement practice, it's good to build these soft guard rails to guide us in the right direction.

Find A Friend Group That Likes to Move

Relationships and people in our lives are some of the most powerful contributors to our desired results and goals. When we surround ourselves with likeminded individuals who live and breathe this movement-based lifestyle, we can't help but be influenced by them. The powerful quote, "You are the average of the 5 people you hang around with, "applies to movement too.

When I grew up in Finland, my life revolved around movement, being active and playing. There was literally no other way for me to live life. Everyone, and I mean EVERYONE around me was active. It was the lifestyle associated with my homeland and remains that way to this day.

The simple truth is that it's a lot easier for me to move than not to move, because of my environment, my mindset, and the people I surround myself with. So, if you want to experience more movement in your life, come and hang out with me for a few days in Tahiti! Or find your own friend group of movers.

Schedule Adventures with The People Who Share Your Passion.

A physical or digital calendar is one of our best non-human friends to add more Movement into our lives. Because *what gets scheduled gets done.* At the end of the day, we remember the adventures and experiences we shared with the people who mattered.

Life becomes so much richer when we experience it in a deep and meaningful way; living life to its fullest. If you look at the richest experiences of your life, I bet they weren't boring and involved some form of Movement.

When We Move, We Feel the Most Alive.

So, it just makes sense to create more of these peak life experiences (PLE's) AND to schedule them into our calendars well ahead of time. This is exactly what one of my clients did during our Coaching. We discovered what his true desires and wants beyond his goals were, and so instead of setting traditional goals, he set himself powerful PLE's!

If you really ask yourself what your goals are for, it's more than likely that the answer is that we actually want these purpose-driven peak life experiences.

Find a Movement Style That Allows Freedom of Expression.

We all have a body that is designed for movement, yet it comes in all different shapes and sizes. Movement that is suitable for one may not be optimal for another.

For me, I know that my body just loves to run due to its long and slim nature. For someone else it might be dancing, yoga or gymnastics. Many men tend to feel a better connection with their bodies when they are pushing or pulling weight. We men typically have a predisposition towards strength training and muscle building.

Women often, but not always, benefit from more subtle movement practices like dancing and yoga. These practices allow them to connect deeply with their femininity.

In order to find the appropriate movement practice, look for signs & feelings of lightness and flow. You can also ask yourself these questions: *What movement discipline comes to you naturally? Where do you feel the most at ease and as your authentic self?*

There you can also express yourself as your unique you. When your sense of time expands or shrinks in your mind you are most likely experiencing flow. The type of movement practice that induces flow is worth pursuing more of.

Make Movement a Part of Your Identity.

As human beings we are movers. We are not intended to be couch potatoes that can barely kneel to play with our children or get out of breath after only a minute of running.

Movement is how we experience the world around us. It also helps us to feel in tune with our bodies and think deeper. When we can fold this movement-based lifestyle into our everyday life, and become a person who moves, we are taking massive leaps in the right direction.

One of the most powerful moves is to build and embody a movement as a part of your Identity. This internal shift becomes a powerful part of your character and how people know you. It's also an empowering inside-out approach that can transform your external circumstances.

Be the person who moves, and you will become the person you are meant to be.

Create your PDF's (Pockets of Deep Flow)

Flow combined with freedom of movement is where we feel the most fully alive. I personally like to be highly intentional about these spaces of time. I call them the *Pockets of Deep Flow*. To start, set up completely uninterrupted, intentional, and purpose driven pockets of time, from a minimum of 1 hour up to a whole day, that allow for maximum experiences of flow.

We are fully immersed in the experience at hand. The separation of self, the boundaries from our internal world to the external world melt as we feel ourselves performing at our highest potential.

These are rich moments to cherish and experience life at higher levels. Our capacity to think, feel, and move grows exponentially. The now famous research from McKinsey Group found that executives in Flow were 500% more productive when in flow versus when out of Flow. ([Citation]).

For me, most if not all of my Peak Life Experiences have involved periods of deep flow and immersive movement. Activities like ultra trail runs up in the mountains, camper van trips in New Zealand without technology, TEDx talks in front of cameras and hundreds of people.

In Short

I am genuinely confident in saying that Flow and Movement are pathways to a richer, deeper and more fulfillment-based life.

When we move, we are and feel the most alive. Movement is a fundamental part of being a human because our natural design is intended to move. Embrace your unique abilities and cherish the freedom of expressing yourself through movement.

How can you make this chapter a reality in your life?

What can you do today to start forward momentum towards movement as a lifestyle?

Who are the people that you need to surround yourself?

What is the support you need?

With the answers to these questions, you can start your movement journey for a better, healthier, and more vibrant you!

CHAPTER 11

Overcoming Personal Limitations

By Jacqueline Power

As a qualified life and business coach I have overcome personal limitations and now I help others to overcome theirs Oprah Winfrey says, "The greatest discovery of all time is that a person can change his future be merely changing his attitude." Overcoming a personal limitation requires some change in thinking, attitude etc so read on and discover different ways of overcoming.

The first is taking a step. You might like to call it baby steps, or a step in the right direction. However you frame it, it is doing something, making forward movement, even if it's only small.

Don't be afraid to set goals that feel unreachable, it's part of stepping out of your comfort zone...we limit ourselves with our thoughts but if you believe in something then thinking big is a helpful way to get there. Starting with small steps means first going for a 10-minute run then setting your goals higher and higher and soon you're running for 60 minutes after a few weeks.

I'm looking at writing a book soon, so my first step is writing this chapter... the biggest goals all start with a single step...as the great Nike quote says..." Just do it" so let me encourage you to embrace the uncomfortable as you take the first steps to the best of your life.

Trusting in yourself is another step. We all have potential, I learnt this as a special ed teacher where the smallest step, which could be simply adding a new word to a ten-word vocabulary was a huge achievement and something to be celebrated. They may seem small steps to some but still steps to reaching their potential.

Sometimes we are too critical of ourselves and we sabotage ourselves with our limiting beliefs "I'm only a secretary, I can't become a CEO" or " Nobody in my family has ever run a business so I definitely can't." Even the friends we surround ourselves with can aid us in our limiting beliefs because of their own.

We all have strengths and weaknesses, if you're not sure what yours are there are quizzes and questionnaires online. I used the VIA Character Strengths Survey and use it with my clients as it is a great place to start and helps overcome the "I don't have any strengths limiting belief."

Trust in yourself and explore your inner potential by doing new things or doing things differently. Take a different turn when driving home and see where it takes you for example. Prove to yourself that you absolutely can handle new challenges and if fact, you're capable of more than you would ever think possible.

Taking steps, even small ones can highlight the fears we have, these are limiting and keep us in our comfort zone. Fear is natural to us and with good reason, however we can let fear inhibit us and prevent our growth. Every time I/we consciously choose to step out of our comfort zone, the next uncomfortable experience becomes less scary, and we see that we can indeed overcome our fears and we can be proud of that overcoming nature we are developing.

Facing your fears shows us that we have the ability to control our emotions and fear is just one perspective of limiting our thinking.

I started my life and business coaching business after qualifying, it was a big step for me as I had grown up believing that "you must have a job." This limiting belief is something that I had to overcome and henceforth "I can have a successful business" is what I replaced the limiting one with.

Follow your passion. This is worth taking time to identify. There's a saying "Build a life you don't need a vacation from." Find different things to do and identify what makes you feel happy, where you feel strong and increase it in your life. My passion is helping people, I started as a teacher but found myself disillusioned then after completing a counselling diploma I was drawn to life coaching which I did and now I live my passion.

Ask the difficult questions. Don't be afraid to do this there are no wrong or stupid questions so ask yourself. And others, the challenging questions and develop the ability to see things form a different angle or perspective. Don't be afraid to ask for feedback, ask without hesitating. Ask yourself "WHY?". Ask how you can improve yourself, why do you do things the way you do. You will find answers within and outside your comfort zone.

Break your routines. I touched on this previously when I suggested taking different routes home. Look at how you can do the things you do the same way daily in a different way e.g. play your brain games or do hobbies at a different time of day. This encourages different thinking; it can be inspirational and gives you the chance to explore who you are in different situations. This can be so liberating and good for personal growth.

Following on from this is trying something new or agreeing to something outside your usual way of being. This could be agreeing to a project which may not totally match your expertise and experience or try a new hobby, a new food. It may or may not work but every new environment, experience, group opens us up to reshaping our thoughts and opening us to different perspectives.

Giving up control and trusting the process is also a way of overcoming personal limitations. As a bit of a control freak myself, I have learnt for my sanity thatI had to learn about what I can and cannot control. My mind, body, emotions, eating, drinking, activities are all within my control however external factors, the "shit happens" events make our lives more complex and believe it or not more interesting. Stepping out of ye olde comfort zone makes you more creative and works beautifully on those limiting self-beliefs because you find new ways of thinking and acting. You extend your limits, explore new ways of handling challenges thus expanding your potential, becoming stronger and opening new growth with endless possibilities.

Be mindful and self-aware. Mindfulness is a state of being, a moment-by-moment awareness of our thoughts, feelings, bodily reactions through a gentle nurturing lens. Being mindful means, you pay attention and accept thoughts and feelings without judging them. A way of having our thoughts tune into what we are sensing in the now of life rather than remembering the past or imagining the future. Bringing a balance to our lives. If you look online there are many methods of growing mindfulness e.g. Wim Hof's method of meditation, cold water exposure, breathing and focus. Other ways are taking time for meditation, journaling and many more.

Before we go on, I will share a way I have found to change thoughts from negative to positive, thoughts that keep us in our comfort zone, those thoughts that limit us personally. I use this personally and with clients. It's a therapy called Cognitive Behaviour Therapy and was started by Albert Ellis who devised Rational Emotive behaviour Therapy (REBT) in 1950'sand in 1960's Aaron T. Beck a psychiatrist researched whether holding negative views could contribute to depression and CBT, a therapy for identifying and challenging unhelpful thoughts was born. CBT helps people identify and challenge unhelpful thoughts then learning alternative thinking patterns and behaviours. The overall goal is to teach the skill of breaking down negative thought patterns like our limiting beliefs and changing them into amor helpful approach to handling daily life.

The first step is identifying the negative thought. For example, "I can't do that I'm too dumb.". step two is becoming aware of the unhelpful thoughts, beliefs and emotions step three is identifying negative or inaccurate thinking step four is reshaping /reframing those thoughts to something more healthy and helpful i.e. with the original thought I'm too dumb becoming I can do that, learning new things helps me grow.

CHAPTER 12

Dealing with External Pressures and Expectations

By Inara Dodhiya

External Expectation: Societal and Familial

Imagine this: You're in the heart of "Peer Pressure Central City", where making downright foolish choices was practically a daily sport. (Are you there yet? Great!) Now, let's talk about Mary – she's the star of our show. She's just waved goodbye to her cushy job because her family insists there's a better one waiting in the big, bustling city. But here's the kicker, folks – Mary had already struck gold with that job! Now, she's knee-deep in the quicksand of societal and familial expectations, all while chasing an illusion. It's like swapping a precious gem for a sack of shiny pebbles. Mary's tale is a head-scratcher, reminding us that sometimes the path to happiness isn't paved with other people's expectations. In a way, we are all Mary, which brings us to the topic of External Expectation from Society and Family, and how we can deal with it.

Expectations can be described as our anticipation that certain events or outcomes will occur. They are the lens through which we perceive how situations will unfold, guided by a blend of factual evidence and personal beliefs. Let's take a closer look and dive into the deep end of societal and familial standards here. We're talking about those unspoken rules, the behavioral do's and don'ts that influence how we fit into our social circles and communities. Stray from these norms, and you might get some eyebrow raises from your peers. But hold on a sec! There's a rebel in every crowd; those brave souls who love to shake things up. Your family has their own set of expectations, which can be as diverse as your crazy aunt's conspiracy theories. From sibling rivalries to parental wisdom, it's a web of beliefs, behaviors, and lifestyle choices that keep you in line with your clan.

Now, imagine understanding and embracing these norms as if you've just mastered the secret handshake to an exclusive club. These expectations are like the invisible ropes guiding our social ship through uncharted waters. So, ahoy, matey! Ready to set sail on this fascinating journey?

In a nutshell, societal and familial expectations act like the subtle referees of our game of life. They're those unspoken hopes and standards set by society and family, quietly guiding us on how to play the game. These invisible referees tell us the rules, define the goals, and even throw in some curveballs to keep things interesting. They have a say in what counts as a "win," be it a specific career, a unique marriage path, or hitting milestones like a pro gamer.

Whether these referees blow the whistle or just give us the side-eye, they profoundly influence how we see ourselves and our fellow players. Navigating this game means understanding these rules and sometimes even challenging them to score our own points on the path to fulfillment. But beware, some societal expectations can be real tough opponents, making you feel like the odd one out.

Exercise: "Referee Reflection": Imagine your life as a game, and societal and familial expectations as the referees guiding your moves. In this exercise, take a reflective journey by creating your personal "Game of Life" board. Draw a path that represents your life, complete with milestones and challenges. Identify areas where societal and familial expectations have influenced your decisions, marked by referee icons.

Now, add alternative paths or "power-ups" that align with your authentic desires, challenging the conventional rules. Reflect on moments when you felt like the odd one out or faced tough opponents. Finally, envision your unique victory, breaking free from expectations. This creative exercise helps you visualize your journey, raise awareness of societal roadblocks, and strategize ways to overcome them, empowering you to play the game of life on your terms.

Are you ready to trade your precious gem for a sack of shiny pebbles, like Mary? Or will you navigate the game of societal and familial expectations with your own play-book?

External Expectations from Society and Family

Society

Picture this: a world where happiness is a 24/7 require-ment. Society insists that life should be an endless parade of grins, like we're all auditioning for a toothpaste com-mercial. But let's get real, we're not cardboard cutouts; we're beautifully flawed humans. It's okay to ride the emotional rollercoaster; it's what makes us, well, us. Now, society often dreams of a Cinderella story when it comes to career success, where there are no limits like a mid-night curfew. They make it sound like you can conquer the professional realm without losing sleep or a chunk of your soul, but newsflash: there's no pumpkin carriage to whisk you away from sacrifices.

Then there's the body image conundrum. Unrealistic beauty standards are everywhere, making us feel like we're prepping for the Victoria's Secret runway. But guess what? You're not a mannequin, you're you, and that's pretty amazing. Embrace those quirks, and remember, you're the masterpiece in a gallery of photocopies.

Then there's the dream of conflict-free relationships; our society's fairy tale that love should be smooth sailing. But let's face it, every rom-com needs a bit of drama. Disagreements are like relationship vitamins; they help you grow stronger together.

Last but not least, the constant productivity myth. The world expects us to be robots, firing on all cylinders 24/7. But guess what? We're not machines, we're humans that deserve Netflix breaks.

Take that break, savor those snacks, and remember, even rocket ships need a pit stop sometimes. Don't let the pressure squeeze the fun out of life!

Family

Ah, the family's quest for the ideal career feels like they've armed themselves with blueprints for your life. Although their intentions are good, persuading someone to excel in a field they'd rather escape is as futile as trying to make a cactus bloom as a tulip. However, amidst this familial crusade, the true treasure hunt lies in discovering your own path.

The rollercoaster continues with the familial pressure to marry by a certain age. After all, who doesn't love the idea of setting a deadline for love? But, in reality, you're not a carton of milk with an expiration date stamped on your forehead. Waiting for the right person is far more rewarding than settling for a partner as ill-suited to you as a swimsuit in a snowstorm. The journey to love is a unique one for each of us, and there's no need to rush it.

Then comes the reproduction pressure – family's favorite sport. It's like they're running a spectator event from the stands, chanting, "Womb-Watch 2023!" But let's be real; the decision to bring "mini-me's" into the world should be as personal as your secret candy stash. No need for a crowd in that delivery room.

And who can forget the "Support the Whole Family" Olympic Games, where you suddenly become their emotional ATM? It's essential to remember that you're not a human-shaped wallet; it's crucial to strike a balance between your own well-being and your family responsibilities. Prioritizing your own happiness and mental health is not a selfish act, but a necessary one.

Lastly, the pursuit of perfection, family-style. Unrealistic expectations about behavior can make you feel like you're expected to be a flawless robot. But the truth is, we're not designed for perfection; we're here to embrace our occasional blunders, much like composing a heartfelt message only to accidentally send it to the wrong person.

Embracing your quirks and imperfections is what makes you uniquely you.

We've experienced the thrilling ride of life's demands, whether it's society pushing for 24/7 happiness or family acting as your life's blueprint. As you consider the external pressures and expectations that may be influencing your life–

What aspects of your own journey toward self-discovery and fulfillment resonate with you the most? How do you envision addressing them in a way that aligns with your authentic self?

With all these unrealistic expectations it's inevitable that we feel a lot of pressure, but recognizing them and addressing them can lead to more understanding and healthier relationships with our family and society. The unrealistic expectations from society and family can indeed exert significant pressure. Research has shown that societal expectations and pressures can contribute to mental health issues, including depression.

Dr. Bharghav Sirivelu, a psychiatrist associated with Apollo 24/7 (2023), states that, "Breaking down gender stereotypes is crucial to free both men and women from the destructive psychological distress."

In the intricate dance of societal expectations, the spotlight often intensifies when it comes to gender roles.

Dr. Bharghav Sirivelu's insights pierce through the haze, highlighting the urgency of dismantling entrenched gender stereotypes. The pressure to conform to predefined notions of masculinity and femininity can be suffocating, affecting not only individual mental health but also perpetuating harmful societal norms. The struggle to fit into these predetermined molds can lead to a profound internal conflict, as individuals grapple with the dissonance between their authentic selves and society's rigid expectations. Unraveling these gender stereotypes becomes a crucial part of the journey toward self-discovery and fulfillment. It involves not only recognizing the external pressures but also questioning and reshaping the internal narratives that have been shaped by societal norms.

As we navigate through the minefield of expectations, it becomes evident that challenging these stereotypes is not just a personal endeavor but a collective act of defiance against a system that perpetuates psychological distress. The path to authenticity involves breaking free from the shackles of gender norms, allowing individuals to embrace their true selves and fostering a society that values diversity and individuality. It's a journey that requires courage, resilience, and a collective commitment to redefine the narrative; one that liberates both men and women from the corrosive effects of rigid gender expectations.

How External Expectations Affect our Internal Expectations

Let's talk a little about how external expectations affect your mental health and self-identity. Imagine life as an arena where external expectations wrestle with your inner world. It's a continuous clash of values, with society and family's desires contending against your own beliefs. Who's the heavyweight champion in this ring? External expectations don't knock politely; they barge in like they own the place, rearranging your mental furniture. You end up feeling like camouflage in your new dress code, blending in when you should be standing out.

However, there's a twist in the tale: as you embrace this chameleon role, your personal growth and happiness take a backseat. They become the overlooked friends, while society and family revel in VIP status. And when you find yourself unable to meet these towering expectations, your self-esteem receives a brutal blow. Doubts about your abilities and worth begin to pour in, disrupting your personal goals.

As for the fear of disappointing both the world and your loved ones? That's the deadly duo. It stifles your true self, immobilizes your dreams, and flings your life goals out the window. You become akin to an approval addict, yearning for validation from others while your own desires gather dust. Falling short of these expectations isn't just an "Oops!" It's a relentless "I'm not good enough" assault on your mental well-being.

The cherry on top? Stress and anxiety, like an eternal to-do list on steroids, are now your close pals. They leave you overwhelmed and frazzled. In the pursuit of making everyone else happy, your relationships start to feel like strangers. Couples even forget why they were together, fearing society's judgment more than nurturing their love. You become the ultimate people-pleaser, leaving your authentic self in the dust.

Exercise: Mirror Monologue. Break free from the approval addiction with the Mirror Monologue. Stand before a mirror, take a deep breath, and share your thoughts, dreams, and aspirations aloud for the next five minutes. Reflect on the impact of external expectations on your self-image, exploring moments where you felt compelled to conform. Acknowledge buried dreams and passions and recognize approval-seeking patterns influenced by societal and familial expectations. This exercise fosters self-awareness, allowing you to confront ingrained narratives and reclaim authenticity. Embrace the opportunity to reconnect with your true self and break free from the chains of external expectations.

Living a life scripted by others leads to an identity crisis. You forget who you truly are, wandering in a fog of confusion. It's like having a personal compass that's lost its way, and it's not doing wonders for your mental well-being. But the plot can twist again.

Balance is the hero of this story; finding the sweet spots between society's applause and your own desires. That's the key to staying true to yourself while keeping the important connections intact. It's the secret sauce for your mental well-being.

Society often subtly influences our thoughts and emotions, molding our personal reasoning without our conscious awareness. This isn't inherently negative, I mean, wouldn't it be pretty weird if a middle-aged man walked right into your favorite restaurant and stripped naked while listening to Hannah Montana on a speaker? Jokes aside, these norms can profoundly affect our choices and beliefs. It's crucial to be aware of the extent to which they shape our lives, some societal norms are norms for a good reason.

While some advantages of societal expectations include facilitating seamless interactions among community members, they don't necessarily guarantee individual purpose. People adhering to these norms can still struggle, while those who deviate might flourish. Societal expectations should be choices individuals make to navigate life, free from coercion or stigma.

So, amidst this epic wrestling match between societal and familial expectations and your true self, here's a question: *To what degree have you recognized the societal influences wrestling with your personal choices and beliefs in the ring of life, and how might achieving equilibrium between external norms and your inner aspirations act as the referee guiding your authentic self and overall well-being?*

Strategies to Combat External Expectations

Picture yourself as the vivid stroke of colour on a canvas of monotony, the unexpected plot twist in the novel of conformity. In this grand play of life, you are the lead character, and the script is yours to write. Let's embark on this journey of being unapologetically you. Imagine this: you're a rare gem in a world of pebbles and your path is unlike anyone else's. It's time to let your uniqueness shine and not dim your light for anyone.

Creating an inner roadmap: Channel your inner philosopher, reflect on your values, desires, and goals. Think of it as your personal roadmap; without it, you're just wandering in the woods. Your dreams and aspirations are unique, and it's essential to understand them fully.

Communication: Now, let's talk turkey. Open, honest conversations with your family and friends are your secret weapon. They need to know the battles you're fighting, and it helps avoid those epic conflicts. Clear communication builds bridges and avoids misunderstandings. It's like drawing your personal force field, or boundaries. These invisible lines will keep your mental and emotional well-being safe from external invaders. You're the gatekeeper, and YOU decide who gets in.

Form your Avengers squad for support: Venture out to chase your passions, my friend, like an intrepid explorer seeking hidden treasure. And remember, your happiness is the ultimate loot. When seeking support, think of it as forming your Avengers squad. Surround yourself with superheroes who've got your back, and don't hesitate to call in Doctor Strange (or a therapist) when needed.

Self-Care Mastery: As you indulge in self-care practices like enjoying a bubble bath or taking a mindful walk, navigating the twists and turns of your journey toward self-discovery and fulfillment, self-care becomes your secret potion against stress. Think of it as your daily spa day, without going bankrupt. Engage in positive affirmations, repeating phrases like "I am resilient and confident" or "I embrace my authentic self," serving as your personal cheerleaders, the ones who'll keep you going even when the game gets tough. You've got this! Become the master of "no," like a Jedi wielding the Force. Guard your time and energy; they're your most precious resources.

As you master the art of self-care and assertively protect your time and energy, consider these strategies as your trusty companions on your journey towards managing external pressures and expectations. Just as our explorer unearths hidden treasures, you, too, are uncovering the gems within yourself. This marks the end of our chapter, but your adventure of self-discovery and fulfillment continues.

Life is a grand carnival, and every small win is your golden ticket to the most exhilarating ride. Step right up, folks, and get ready to celebrate your unique journey as the star of this spectacular show. It's time for a standing ovation, and the confetti is just the beginning.

Alright, fellow adventurers, it's time to chart your own path. But, have you ever stopped to ponder: *Are you the superhero in your own story, or are you playing a sidekick in someone else's script?*

Success Stories

Devin, 29 yrs: Overcoming chronic depression, Devin shattered societal norms by pursuing his passion for music instead of succumbing to the expectations of a traditional career. Despite the clash between his family's desire for stability and his dream of becoming a musician, Devin persevered through late-night gigs, proving that the path to success is often unconventional. His journey, far from an overnight triumph, demonstrates the value of staying true to oneself and navigating the challenges to realize one's dreams.

Miss Rania, 22 yrs: In a courageous act of self-liberation, Rania found the strength to divorce her abusive husband after enduring three years of physical assault. Breaking free from the fear of societal judgment, she boldly declares, "I no longer care! I truly feel free." Rania's story challenges the stereotype of failure, showcasing resilience and the pursuit of personal well-being above conforming to societal expectations.

In the spirit of Devin and Miss Rania's courageous journeys, let me pose this question: *What's one external expectation you've overcome to pursue your own path towards happiness?*

Conclusion

To sum it up, life's a wild rollercoaster, and societal and familial expectations can sometimes feel like seatbelts on this ride; necessary, but they can pinch and squeeze and make you feel restricted. We've all been there, trying to fit into molds that aren't meant for us, like Cinderella's stepsisters trying to force their feet into the glass slipper. But guess what? Glass slippers are a rarity, and we've got to find our comfortable shoes.

Remember, it's okay to follow your path. Life isn't one-size-fits-all, and that's the beauty of it. Don't let external expectations steer your ship, you're the captain.

In the end, embracing your individuality and finding a balance between societal norms and personal freedom is the sweet spot. Like a well-baked pie, life should be a perfect blend of delicious and satisfying.

So, now that we've navigated the maze of external expectations, tell me, what's the most daring dream you'd chase if the weight of society and family didn't matter?

Stay authentic, stay true, and keep enjoying every bite of your journey. Cheers to being you!

Wait! One last question and let's spice it up a bit – *If external expectations were a dish, what would it taste like, and would you still take a bite?*

Now, Bye for real, and Goodluck.

~*Inara Dodhiya.*

Like what you read? Learn more about me and my services at http://www.inaradodhiya.com.

CHAPTER 13:

EMBRACING CHANGE AND UNCERTAINTY

By Peter McGee

Born, raised, and living on Vancouver Island, on the West Coast of Canada, I feel that a sailing analogy is always a good place to start when exploring nuanced, layered topics such as this.

If I were to plan a sailing trip from the city of Victoria, British Columbia, on the southern tip of Vancouver Island, across the Salish Sea to the city of Vancouver, I could make an incredibly detailed list of steps. Every step, from packing the sailboat, to releasing the dock lines, raising the fenders, and all the way to docking at one of the many beautiful marinas in Vancouver. If I were to generate the most painstakingly detailed list imaginable, I could hand that list to someone with zero sailing experience, and they could certainly make the journey without issue, right?

Of course the answer is, no. But why not? Simply put, planning out and following every step in a plan only works when either you control the variables, or the variables are unchanging. Even if an inexperienced sailor follows every step perfectly, what will happen when the wind changes? What will happen if the seas become rough? What will happen if there's no room to moor in Vancouver? Sailing is like life: The only way to navigate with confidence, to get where you're going, and to enjoy the journey along the way, is to develop the skill of embracing change and uncertainty. And the only way to do that is with practice.

Change and uncertainty are constants in our lives. No matter how careful we are, and how in control of our circumstances we feel, unplanned events will visit us. The wind will change, and not always in our favor. Our ability to navigate these challenges is dictated by the meanings we attach to them, and more specifically, how those meanings impact our sense of personal identity.

Our personal identity is a complex mix of what we believe in, what we value, and how we view ourselves. It also includes the roles we play, the dreams we chase, and the labels we wear. When life throws us a curveball or we're faced with the unknown, this sense of self shapes how we make sense of it all.

For those who stick to a fixed image of themselves, any change or unpredictability might feel like it's shaking the very core of who they think they are. In other words, stick too close to the list of sailing steps, and you won't be prepared for the inevitable changes that will force you to deviate from that list.

Similarly, those who consider themselves completely adaptable and ready for anything can experience identity crises when faced with unforeseen challenges that they can't handle. In other words, without the life experience and practice in navigating hard conditions, throwing the list of steps overboard could lead to disaster. The goal is to become a skilled sailor (of life), with a solid plan, and the wherewithal to know when and how to deviate from the plan and improvise.

Change, even when unwelcome, has an innate capacity to foster personal growth. When we confront new situations, we are compelled to adapt and develop new skills. This process of adaptation not only equips us with enhanced abilities, but also builds our resilience and flexibility. It challenges us to think outside our usual parameters and to discover hidden potential.

Personal growth through change can include increased self-confidence, improved problem-solving skills, and a greater capacity for innovation. Consider, for example, Steve Jobs' departure and return to Apple. In 1985, Steve Jobs was ousted from Apple, the company he co-founded. This unexpected change forced Jobs to reflect on his approach and leadership style. During his time away, Jobs founded NeXT and Pixar, experiencing both failure and success. When he returned to Apple in 1997, he brought a new perspective and innovative ideas. This period of personal growth for Jobs contributed to the development of iconic products like the iMac, iPod, iPhone, and iPad, revolutionizing the tech industry.

Change nudges us out of our comfort zones, forcing us to learn, grow, and evolve. By embracing change, we open ourselves up to a world of possibilities for self-improvement and development.

Of course, this is easier said than done, and more palatable in reflection after the storm. Shortly after my father died two years ago, the message "just embrace the change, it's good for you" would've certainly fallen flat. Several months ago, when my house burned down 3 days prior to the finalization of the sale to the new would-be buyers (true story), I would've found little comfort in being told of the benefits I'd experience in my confidence as a result. Understanding the value of embracing change is more of a daily meditation than an in-the-moment painkiller.

Our self-identity acts as a lens through which we interpret the world and our place in it. When our identity is rigid and fixed, we are more prone to resist change and feel threatened by uncertainty. We might perceive change as a direct challenge to our identity, instigating feelings of insecurity, fear, and even self-doubt. In such cases, a person might cling to the familiar, shunning new experiences or opportunities for personal growth.

Conversely, an adaptable self-identity rooted in a growth mindset allows us to view change as an opportunity for learning, self-improvement, and evolution. Such a mindset is characterized by a belief in one's capacity to develop new skills and abilities, which leads to resilience in the face of change. Those with a growth mindset understand that their self-identity is not fixed and that they can shape it over time.

For a period of my career, I found myself providing career coaching for high school students. In pitching my approach to the students, their instructors, and in some cases their parents, I would often use the sailing analogy used at the beginning of this chapter. The biggest problem with high school career planning, as I see it, is that students are being encouraged to select a job, and reverse engineer the steps to get into that job. For example, if a grade 11 student states that they want to pursue a career as a lawyer, a few things happen. Usually, their family gets excited! "Lawyer, how impressive!" A list of steps is generated, including grade 12 classes to enroll in as prerequisites for their undergraduate degree. That undergraduate degree needs to lend itself well to a law graduate program. And, at some point, 'feelers' will need to be put out with various law firms in order to secure an articling position, before passing the bar exam and ultimately becoming a certified lawyer.

"So, what's wrong with this plan, Peter?"

The plan is fine. However, it's vulnerable to a great deal of uncertainty. Here are two questions I'd have for our young lawyer-hopeful:

1. How much do you actually know about what lawyers do?
2. What is uniquely appealing to you about that description of their working lives?

Arbitrarily reverse engineering the job title "Lawyer" is similar to being given a to-do list of sailing across the sea, and setting sail without context or experience. The reason those two questions are so important is that they help to provide a bearing, not simply a destination. By identifying WHY we're making the trip, we're actually priming ourselves to better adapt when things inevitably go off course. The worst thing that happens (and it happens a lot), is that someone spends 8 years in post secondary school, and takes on enormous loan debt, only to discover upon starting work at a law firm that they never really wanted to be a lawyer at all. They simply followed the steps they were given, only to look back years later and realize they've been sailing in the wrong direction the entire time.

Change, both welcome and unwelcome, is an inevitable truth of life. To weather those unplanned storms, we must have a firm grasp on our bearing. We must secure our identity to a purpose, not an outcome.

Consider an unwanted change that's been thrust upon you; an event that threw your life into chaos. If you had tied your identity to whatever outcome had been derailed by that event, you will have undergone immense stress, even existential crises. However, tying our sense of self to our underlying principles and mission will allow us to pivot when the moment calls for it. To paraphrase Anthony Robbins, what matters is what we focus on, what it means, and what we're going to do about it.

How to Cultivate an Adaptable Self-Identity

To develop a growth mindset and a more adaptable self-identity, take these practical steps:

1. **Embrace a Learning Orientation**: Adopt a mindset that values the process of learning over the end result. Understand that challenges and setbacks are opportunities for growth.

2. **Embrace Failure as a Stepping Stone to Success**: Recognize that setbacks and failures are part of the journey toward personal development. Instead of seeing them as reflections of your identity, view them as valuable lessons.

3. **Challenge Fixed Beliefs**: Identify and challenge fixed beliefs about your abilities and potential. Ask

yourself whether these beliefs are based on evidence or merely assumptions..

4. **Cultivate a Sense of Curiosity:** Embrace change and uncertainty with a curious and open mindset. Ask questions, seek new experiences, and view the unknown as an opportunity for exploration.

The relationship between self-identity and our approach to change and uncertainty is undeniable. A fixed self-identity often leads to resistance and fear, while an adaptable self-identity rooted in a growth mindset enables us to embrace change and uncertainty with flexibility and resilience. Cultivating a growth mindset is a powerful tool for personal development, enabling us to navigate the unpredictable landscape of life with enthusiasm and a sense of self that is open to constant evolution.

Finally, Some Things You Can Actually Do TODAY

Mindfulness and meditation are powerful tools for reducing anxiety and navigating uncertainty. These practices involve being present in the moment, acknowledging emotions without judgment, and cultivating a sense of inner peace. By focusing on the now, individuals can lessen anxiety about the future.

Mindfulness can be integrated into daily life through exercises like deep breathing and guided meditations.

These practices help you stay grounded and centered, even in the face of uncertainty. They promote self-awareness and emotional regulation, enabling you to better cope with stress and anxiety.

I engage in a daily practice of meditative breathwork. Beyond the clear physiological benefits, I've found (as have millions of others over thousands of years) that the process helps me to clarify my purpose, my bearing, my gratitudes, and my core values. As a result, it's provided me with the strength and perspective I need to navigate life's changes and challenges.

Here's a short step-by-step process to get you started:

1. Try a breathwork or meditation class near you.
2. Commit to writing in a journal everyday for 2 weeks, and focus your entries on your gratitudes and resentments (as these are opposite forces).
3. Increase your water intake, and limit your carbohydrate and sugar intake.
4. If you're not already physically active, take 20-30 minutes a day to walk, run or some other form of exercise to increase your heart-rate.
5. After 2 weeks, come back to this chapter and read it again. Also, reflect on your journal entries, and note any changes in your mindset.

Support Networks and Professional Help

Handling uncertainty can be a tough journey, but it doesn't have to be a lonely one. Having a strong support network of friends, family, or peers can be a source of comfort and guidance. Sharing your concerns and seeking advice from those who care about you can be really reassuring. Their presence can remind you that you're not alone in your struggles.

Sometimes, you might need professional help. When anxiety becomes too much and starts to interfere with your daily life, talking to a therapist or counselor can be incredibly helpful. These experts offer evidence-based strategies to manage anxiety and give you the tools to navigate uncertainty better.

Coping with uncertainty is a skill that you can develop and improve. By using practical tips for managing uncertainty, practicing mindfulness and relaxation techniques, and building a support network or seeking professional help, you can regain a sense of control and emotional well-being when faced with life's unpredictability. These coping strategies can empower you to confront uncertainty with resilience and confidence, ultimately turning it from a challenge into an opportunity for personal growth and strength.

Happy sailing!

CHAPTER 14:

Goal Setting with Purpose and Intention

By Warren Miles-Pickup, Co-Founder Pixel Publishing

In the realm of personal development, goal setting is often lauded as the first stepping stone to success.

However, many find themselves in a perplexing cycle where goals, regardless of their clarity or ambition, fail to resonate on a deeper, more meaningful level.

This misalignment, unnoticed by many, is a critical hindrance. The challenge lies not in the act of setting goals but in infusing these goals with genuine purpose and intention. It's akin to a ship with a rudder but no compass; the potential to move is there, but the direction lacks clarity and conviction. By understanding the underlying issues in traditional goal setting, we can begin to approach our objectives with a more insightful, purpose-driven mindset.

Personal Introduction: Warren Miles-Pickup

Now, allow me to introduce myself. I'm Warren Miles-Pickup, and while my background as a marketing strategist and business owner might not immediately align with life coaching, the parallels between successful marketing strategies and effective personal goal-setting are striking. I have been fortunate to use my goal-setting strategies to accomplish some incredible achievements:

1. **Innovative Marketing and Sales Campaigns:** I've spearheaded numerous successful marketing and sales campaigns, significantly boosting brand visibility and customer engagement for various clients, including selling over 2 billion dollars worth of products in my career.

2. **Business Growth:** Under my leadership, my companies have seen substantial growth; expanding their client base and increasing revenue consistently over the years. I was awarded numerous top honors by Wealth Professional Magazine, Wealth Professional Awards, Sun Life Financial, and Million Dollar Round Table for my business growth successes.

3. **Strategic Partnerships:** I've successfully established key partnerships, enhancing business offerings and creating mutual growth opportunities for all those who have worked with me.

4. **Thought Leadership**: I'm recognized as a thought leader in marketing and sales, frequently contributing insights and strategies to industry discussions.
5. **Client Successes**: My tailored marketing strategies have led to remarkable successes for clients, including increased market share and enhanced brand reputation.

Throughout my career, I've learned that the most impactful goals are those set with a clear understanding of one's personal and professional aspirations, mirroring the tailored approaches we use in targeted marketing and sales campaigns. This chapter draws on my experience to offer insights into setting goals that are not only attainable but also deeply aligned with your personal values and ambitions.

Having said all of that, welcome to the journey of transforming your aspirations into reality!

This chapter isn't just about setting goals; it's about embedding them with purpose and intention into every aspect of your life.

In our fast-paced world, we often find ourselves setting targets based on societal norms or fleeting desires. But true fulfillment lies in goals that resonate with our deepest values and aspirations. Here, we'll unravel the intricate tapestry of practical goal setting, exploring how to align your objectives with your true self. You'll learn not just to set goals but to set the right ones that motivate, inspire, and lead to genuine achievement. It's a path less traveled, certainly, but one that promises a more fulfilling destination.

Let's begin this transformative journey together, where each goal is a stepping stone to a life lived with purpose and passion.

The Essence of Purposeful Goal Setting

Purposeful goal setting transcends the mere listing of aspirations and dreams; it involves embedding your goals with profound personal significance and reinforcing your ambitions to accomplish them. This section delves into the heart of what makes a goal truly purposeful:

1. **Understanding 'Purpose' in Goals:** Purpose acts as the soul of a goal, giving it life and direction. It's about identifying what truly matters to you beyond external influences or temporary desires. Societal expectations have a way of creeping into our purpose without us noticing and watering down their true meaning.

2. **Aligning Goals with Core Values:** A purposeful goal is in harmony with your core values. This alignment ensures that your goals truly reflect who you are and what you stand for, leading to more profound satisfaction and fulfillment.

3. **The Power of 'Why':** Every purposeful goal has a strong 'why' behind it. We will explore the importance of understanding the underlying reasons for your goals, which fuels motivation and resilience in the face of inevitable challenges.

4. **Long-term Vision:** Purposeful goals contribute to a broader vision for your life. They aren't just about immediate achievements but are stepping stones towards a larger, more meaningful life narrative. Reverse engineering your goals helps to ensure they align appropriately with the life you want to live.

5. **The Role of Introspection:** We'll discuss the importance of self-reflection in identifying purposeful goals. Understanding your passions, strengths, and life experiences is crucial in this process.

By the end of this section, you will have a deeper understanding of how to set goals that are not only achievable but also profoundly rewarding and aligned with your personal journey.

1. Understanding 'Purpose' in Goals

The Heart of Your Goals: The essence of 'purpose' in goal setting lies in its power to breathe life and direction into your deeply personal objectives. It's about diving deep into your personal values and identifying what truly matters to you, distinct from the noise of external influences and fleeting desires. This process requires introspection and honesty, peeling back the layers of societal expectations that often subconsciously influence our choices. By focusing on what genuinely resonates with your core beliefs and long-term aspirations, your goals become more than just items on a to-do list; they transform into meaningful pursuits that reflect your true self.

Imagine a sculptor working on a block of marble. To an outsider, it's just a stone, but to the sculptor, it holds a deeply personal vision of the potential of that simple block of marble. The sculpture takes form as they chisel away, guided not just by skill but by a connection to what the marble intrinsically represents. This process mirrors purposeful goal setting. The sculptor must ignore external opinions about what the sculpture should be and instead focus on their own vision. Each strike is intentional, each decision guided by personal values and the deep-seated meaning of the artwork. Similarly, when setting goals, we must carve away the layers of external expectations and fleeting desires to reveal goals that truly resonate with our core beliefs and aspirations, transforming them from mere ambitions into expressions of our true selves.

Societal Influences and Personal Truths: Societal expectations can subtly infiltrate our sense of purpose, leading us to chase goals that don't align with our authentic selves. It's easy to fall into the trap of pursuing objectives that seem right in the eyes of others – whether it's a prestigious job, a certain lifestyle, or material achievements. However, such goals often lack staying power because they don't fulfill our innermost desires and needs. The key is to differentiate between what society deems important and what genuinely brings you fulfillment and joy.

Crafting Goals with Soul: To set goals with purpose, it's essential to engage in consistent self-reflection. Ask yourself what successes have brought you the most satisfaction in the past and why. Understand the themes and values that emerge from these reflections. This process isn't about rejecting external influences outright but rather about filtering and aligning them with your true personal values and aspirations. When your goals are rooted in this deep sense of purpose, they become powerful motivators, guiding you toward a life that's both successful on the outside and richly rewarding on the inside.

2. Aligning Goals with Core Values

Aligning your goals with your core values is fundamental in creating a life that is not only successful but deeply fulfilling. This alignment ensures that your goals accurately represent who you are and who you genuinely aspire to be, rather than a reflection of external influences. When goals are in sync with your core values, they feel more authentic and achievable, leading to a sense of satisfaction that goes beyond mere accomplishment.

Furthermore, this congruence between goals and values acts as a powerful motivator. It provides a clear sense of direction and purpose, making the journey towards achieving these goals more meaningful and enjoyable. It's about creating a life that resonates with your deepest beliefs and passions, leading to a richer, more fulfilling experience. When your core values guide your daily actions and long-term aspirations, you create a harmonious and purpose-driven life.

3. The Power of 'Why'

The 'why' behind each goal is its lifeblood, providing a deep-seated reason that goes beyond surface-level desires. Understanding this 'why' is crucial because it fuels both motivation and resilience in the face of opposition. When you're clear about why a goal matters to you, it becomes more than just an objective; it becomes a mission, imbued with personal significance. This understanding fosters a strong emotional connection to the goal, driving you forward even when challenges arise. It's this connection that sustains your efforts and resilience, turning obstacles into stepping stones rather than roadblocks, and making the journey towards your goal as rewarding as the achievement itself.

Consider a mountaineer aiming to summit Mount Everest. This challenging endeavor requires immense physical and mental preparation. The 'why' for the mountaineer might be a lifelong dream of conquering the world's highest peak, a tribute to a loved one, or a personal test of endurance and willpower. This deep-rooted reason becomes a source of strength, pushing them through grueling training, harsh weather, and treacherous climbs. When the climb gets tough, their 'why' keeps them moving forward, turning each step into a testament to their dedication and resolve.

My amazing wife Rachel had a goal to climb to the base camp of Mount Everest and for her 30th birthday, she did just that. This climb surpasses 5,000 meters of elevation and has been known to take the lives of unprepared adventurers through any number of ever-present dangers. During her climb, elevation sickness took over her body. She recounts losing control of her balance, vision, and bladder as she climbed ever higher. While walking up pathways barely wide enough for a single person, she would pin herself to the walls of the mountain as enormous yaks would push past her, a single misstep resulting in a dramatic fall to one's end. The challenges she faced were numerous, but her deep and intrinsic connection to her goals, being able to inspire her children with the belief that they can accomplish anything, drove her to the eventual success of climbing the base camp of Mount Everest. Her "Why" was her driving force.

4. Long-term Vision

Purposeful goals are akin to book chapters that compose a compelling life story. They go beyond immediate gratification, forming a narrative that unfolds over time. These goals act as milestones, marking progress in a more extensive journey that spans years or even a lifetime. By focusing on long-term vision, you're not just achieving individual goals; you're gradually building the life you aspire to live. This approach ensures each goal contributes meaningfully to your overall life plan, harmonizing short-term achievements with your long-term aspirations.

Reverse engineering your goals is a strategic approach to ensure they align with your broader life vision. By envisioning the life you want in the future, you can work backward to identify the steps needed to get there. This process helps in setting milestones that are achievable and significant in the grand scheme of your life. It's about connecting the dots between your daily actions and the future you envision, ensuring each goal is a deliberate step towards creating the life narrative you desire.

5. The Role of Introspection

Introspection plays a pivotal role in identifying goals that are not only achievable but also deeply fulfilling. This self-reflective process involves delving into your own psyche to understand your true passions, strengths, and experiences. It's about exploring what genuinely excites and motivates you, recognizing your unique skills, and re-calling the life experiences that have shaped your per-spective and aspirations. This journey inward is essential for setting goals that are authentically aligned with who you are at your core.

Moreover, introspection allows you to identify patterns in your past successes and challenges, offering insights into what truly drives you. It's a process of uncovering your personal truths and using them as the compass for future goal setting. By understanding what has historically brought you joy, fulfillment, and a sense of accomplish-ment, you can craft goals that not only propel you forward but also bring a profound sense of satisfaction and pur-pose to your life.

Setting Intentions for Success

Intention is the compass that guides your journey to-wards achieving your goals. It's not just about what you want to achieve, but how you plan to achieve it and why it matters. This section explores the crucial role of inten-tion in goal setting:

1. **Defining Intention in Goals:** Intentions are the mind-ful, deliberate approaches we take toward achieving our goals. They shape our daily actions and attitudes.

2. **Crafting Clear Intentions**: Learn how to define clear, actionable intentions that provide a roadmap for achieving your goals.

3. **Consistency and Commitment**: Setting intentions requires consistency. This part discusses how to stay committed to your intentions, even when faced with obstacles.

4. **Mindfulness and Reflection**: Incorporate mindfulness practices to maintain focus on your intentions and reflect on your progress.

5. **Aligning Actions with Intentions**: Ensuring that your daily actions and decisions are aligned with your set intentions is key to successful goal achievement.

Defining intention in your goals starts with precise, mindful planning. This first step involves identifying what you truly want to achieve and going beyond surface-level desires to uncover deeper motivations. It's about asking yourself why these goals matter to you and how they align with your core values. This clarity in understanding the 'why' behind your goals forms the foundation of your intentions.

Once you've defined your goals and their underlying reasons, the next step is to translate this understanding into actionable intentions. This involves setting specific, measurable, and realistic steps that will guide your daily actions toward achieving these goals. These intentions should be focused on the outcome and the journey – how you plan to approach challenges, the attitudes you'll adopt, and the values you'll uphold along the way.

Lastly, implementing these intentions requires a commitment to mindfulness and consistency. It's about continually aligning your daily actions with your set intentions. This can involve regular self-reflection, tracking your progress (journaling), and adjusting your approach as necessary. By staying mindful and consistent, your intentions become an integrated part of your journey towards your goals, shaping not just what you achieve, but also how you achieve it.

Practical Steps in Goal Setting

In the journey of setting purposeful goals, the initial step involves a deep dive into your aspirations across various facets of life, such as career, personal development, health, and relationships. This stage is about distilling these aspirations into clear, well-defined goals. These goals must be articulated with precision and specificity, making them tangible and measurable. Writing them down further solidifies your commitment and provides a tangible reference point.

Aligning these goals with your personal values and intentions forms the next critical phase. Each goal must be scrutinized through the lens of your core values to ensure they truly represent what matters most to you. This alignment extends to the incorporation of your intentions within each goal, ensuring that every objective is not just an end in itself but also a reflection of your broader life aspirations. Regular reevaluation and adjustment of your goals are essential, allowing them to evolve alongside your changing values and life circumstances, thereby maintaining their relevance and resonance with your personal journey.

Here is a practical activity to align goals with personal values:

Values and Goals Alignment Worksheet:

- Create a two-column worksheet. In the first column, list your core values (e.g., creativity, family, health).
- In the second column, list your current goals.
- For each goal, write a brief statement on how it aligns with one or more of your core values.
- If a goal doesn't align with any value, reconsider its relevance and either modify it or replace it with a goal that aligns better with your values.

This exercise helps in ensuring that your goals are not just aspirations but reflections of what you truly value in life.

Overcoming Challenges

In the journey of goal setting, encountering obstacles is not an if but a when. These challenges, ranging from dwindling motivation and unrealistic expectations to external distractions, can significantly hinder progress toward achieving your goals. Understanding why these obstacles arise is the first step in overcoming them. It's crucial to recognize that these challenges are a normal part of the process and can be tackled by employing the right strategies.

To overcome these obstacles, adopting a practical approach is essential. For instance, when motivation wanes, breaking down larger goals into smaller, manageable tasks can reignite your drive and provide a quick sense of accomplishment releasing that dopamine that your brain is craving. Adjusting expectations to more achievable levels can also prevent feelings of being overwhelmed and disappointed.

Maintaining focus on your long-term goals is another crucial aspect. Regular reviews of your goals, seeking support and accountability from peers, mentors, or family members, and utilizing tracking tools can help keep you on course. Additionally, adapting your goals to align with changing circumstances is not only practical but necessary. This flexibility ensures that your goals remain relevant and achievable even as your life inevitably evolves. By embracing practical strategies, you can navigate through the hurdles of goal setting and stay committed to your path of personal growth and achievement.

Exercises and Actionable Tips

1.) *Goal Mapping with Intention Exercise*

1. **Prepare Your Tools**: Grab a large sheet of paper or a whiteboard and some colored markers.

2. **Set Your Main Goal**: Write down your primary goal in the center. Make it as specific as possible.

3. **Break It Down**: Around this primary goal, write down smaller, actionable steps that lead to achieving this goal. These should be straightforward, manageable tasks.

4. **Add Intentions**: Write a short statement of intention next to each step. For example, if a step is to 'Attend Networking Events,' the intention might be 'To connect with like-minded professionals and learn from them.'

5. **Reflect on Values**: Ensure each step aligns with your core values. If a step doesn't resonate with your values, reconsider its place in your goal map.

6. **Visualize the Path**: Use arrows or lines to connect the steps, showing the path you envision taking toward your goal.

7. **Review and Adjust**: Regularly review your goal map, adjusting as your journey evolves.

This exercise helps in visualizing the journey towards your goal, ensuring each step is intentional and aligned with your values.

2.) Applying Purposeful Goal-Setting Principles Daily Exercise

1. **Morning Reflection**: Begin each day with a 5-minute reflection on your main goal and its purpose. Remind yourself why this goal is important to you.

2. **Daily Goals Aligned with Long-Term Vision**: Set small, daily goals that are steps towards your larger goal. For instance, if your long-term goal is to write a book, a daily goal could be to write a specific number of words or brainstorm ideas for a chapter.

3. **Evening Review**: End your day with a brief review of your progress. Acknowledge what you achieved and where you could improve, keeping your long-term vision in mind.

This routine helps to keep your daily actions aligned with your long-term goals, ensuring that every day moves you closer to your overarching aspirations.

3.) Maintaining Momentum and Assessing Progress Exercise

1. **Weekly Check-Ins**:

Schedule a set time each week to review progress towards your goals. Use this time to reflect on what you've accomplished and what challenges you faced.

2. **Celebrate Small Wins**:

Recognize and celebrate small achievements along the way. This could be as simple as treating yourself to something special or sharing your progress with a friend or mentor.

3. **Track Progress with Tools:**

Utilize apps or tools designed for goal tracking. These can help you visualize your progress and stay on track.

4. **Set Milestones:**

Break down your goal into smaller milestones. Celebrate reaching these milestones as a way to maintain motivation.

This activity helps in sustaining motivation, regularly assessing progress, and making necessary adjustments to your goals and strategies.

Conclusion

As we conclude this chapter, let's revisit the essential insights we've explored. We delved into the significance of aligning goals with personal values and intention's critical role in successful goal setting. These concepts are not just strategies but gateways to a fulfilling life journey.

I encourage you to embrace this approach to goal setting wholeheartedly. The journey might be challenging, but the rewards of living a life aligned with your true purpose and intentions are immeasurable. Start applying the strategies and exercises we discussed and embrace the transformative journey ahead.

Reflect on your personal growth journey as you implement these principles.

Remember, goal setting is a continuous process of self-improvement and learning. As you move forward, keep an open mind to adapting and learning, knowing that each step you take is a step towards a more fulfilling life. Your journey doesn't end here; it evolves with each goal you set and every dream you pursue.

I challenge you to embrace the journey of intentional goal-setting!

Start today by applying one principle or exercise from this chapter. Remember, every small step is a leap toward your dreams. Share your journey with others, seek feedback, and stay committed. Your future self will thank you for the decisions you make today. Let's transform aspirations into achievements. Are you ready to take the first step towards a life filled with purpose and intention?

CHAPTER 15

Building Meaningful Relationships; Cultivating Connections that Nourish the Soul

By Sharon Piel

Human beings are inherently social creatures; we thrive when we make meaningful connections with others, contributing to our sense of fulfillment and personal growth. Having a tribe - a group of friends or individuals who share the same interests, values and beliefs as us, gives us a sense of belonging, support and shared identity, contributing to our overall well-being.

However, relationships are inherently complex due to the unique temperaments and diverse life experiences we bring to each interaction. So, the question becomes, how can we cultivate meaningful relationships and deepen our connections with others when miscommunication and misunderstandings can so easily arise, leading to conflict and possible damage to our relationships? I firmly believe that the path to this lies in the development of Emotional

Intelligence, which plays a pivotal role in our ability to understand and manage ourselves and our relationships.

Daniel Goleman, a psychologist who popularized the concept of emotional intelligence, conducted extensive research and wrote several books that discuss the impact of EQ on various aspects of life, including relationships. Other researchers like John Mayer and Peter Salovey have also contributed significantly to understanding the role of emotional intelligence in interpersonal connections. Studies have shown that individuals with higher emotional intelligence tend to communicate more effectively. They can express their feelings and needs clearly, leading to better understanding and reduced misunderstandings in relationships.

Emotional Intelligence (EQ) encompasses our capacity to comprehend our own emotions, behaviors, and their impact on others, as well as our ability to understand and manage our relationships. Emotional Intelligence consists of four fundamental components: Self-Awareness, Self-Management, Social Awareness, and Relationship Management.

Self-Awareness: The Foundation of Emotional Intelligence

Self-awareness is the bedrock of emotional intelligence. It involves recognizing our emotions and how they influence others, understanding our strengths and weaknesses, and identifying our values and responsibilities, both in our personal and professional lives. True self-awareness is about confidently embracing who we are, both personally and professionally. It serves as the initial step in changing our behavior or attitude, and influencing how we engage with others.

Individuals with low self-awareness may inadvertently hurt others due to a lack of awareness of their emotional triggers. They often repeat the same mistakes and struggle to accept constructive feedback. On the other hand, those with high self-awareness understand their emotional triggers, know what they feel and why, recognize their strengths and weaknesses, approach life with humility, and readily accept and learn from feedback.

Enhancing self-awareness is a pivotal step in strengthening our relationships with others. To build self-awareness, engage in self-reflection, acknowledge your true feelings, and connect with your emotions on a visceral level. This enables you to exert control over your reactions and engage in self-regulation effectively. Self-awareness is about knowing and understanding your own emotions, beliefs, principles, values (what is important to you), your motivations, thinking patterns, and attitudes. Self-awareness also brings awareness to your tendencies to react to certain situations, what you want out of life and who you aspire to be.

To facilitate self-awareness, consider asking yourself these reflective questions:

- *What impression do I want people to have of me?*
- *How do my actions align with my self-perception?*
- *Is it more important to be liked or to be authentic?*
- *What legacy do I want to leave?*
- *Which behaviors in others tend to provoke my emotional responses?*
- *Why do these behaviors upset me?*
- *Is preserving the relationship more important than being right?*

Self-Management: The Art of Emotional Regulation

Self-Management, or Self-Regulation, pertains to our ability to maturely manage our emotions through restraint and self-control. It entails taking responsibility for our behavior, holding ourselves accountable for our actions, and preventing impulsive reactions. For example, when triggered emotionally, take a pause, and take deep breaths, affording you the opportunity to respond with calmness rather than react impulsively, which can potentially damage the relationship.

Consider these reflective questions for self-management:

- *What strategies can I employ to maintain emotional composure?*
- *How can I prevent impulsive reactions in emotional situations?*
- *In what ways can I hold myself accountable for my actions?*
- *What practices help me maintain self-control in challenging moments?*

Social Awareness: Building Trust and Rapport

In addition to understanding ourselves, it's crucial to understand others and hone our social skills. Social awareness encompasses our capacity to build trust, establish rapport, understand others, and resolve conflicts. While coaches often emphasize the importance of building rapport with clients, it's equally essential to apply these principles to other aspects of our lives, both personally and professionally.

Effective communication plays a significant role in building and maintaining successful relationships. Communication skills encompass listening, speaking, observing, and empathizing. There are three primary communication styles: Passive, Aggressive, and Assertive.

Passive individuals may appear timid and often feel unheard and taken advantage of, leading to frustration and resentment. Aggressive communicators come across as pushy and may dominate conversations, potentially making others feel disrespected. Assertive communicators exude confidence, resilience, and respect, allowing individuals to express their opinions, feelings, and disagreements respectfully, while confidently offering suggestions and ideas. By practicing self-awareness, we can better understand our own communication style, as well as that of others.

Another vital skill is active listening. Active listening plays a pivotal role in nurturing relationships. Humans yearn to feel seen and heard, making active listening an essential element of connection and trust-building. Building trust stands as a cornerstone in cultivating meaningful relationships. Practice verbal active listening skills by paraphrasing, using short verbal affirmations, asking open-ended questions, showing empathy, sharing similar experiences, and recalling relevant information. Non-verbal active listening skills include maintaining eye contact, nodding, smiling, and avoiding distracting movements.

Relationship Management: Managing Conflict with Empathy

Conflict is an inherent part of any relationship, arising when individuals hold differing perspectives, or have disagreements revolving around matters of importance or unmet expectations. Two types of conflict exist: Relationship conflict, characterized by anger and blame; and Task conflict, focused on problem-solving rather than assigning blame. Recognizing the difference between relationship conflict, which damages relationships, and task conflict, which focuses on problem-solving, is essential. When engaging in conflict resolution, managing one's emotions and responding with empathy is vital.

Here are some reflective questions to ask yourself about how you engage in conflict:

- *Do I avoid conflict?*
- *Do I give in to others?*
- *Do I try to get my own way?*
- *Do I work together with the other person to find a solution?*
- *Have I ever experienced a positive outcome from a conflict?*
- *What happened that made that conflict turn out positive. Example: finding a better solution, improved relationship with the other person.*

- How do I generally deal with conflict? Do I avoid it or respond aggressively?

- Think about recent conflicts you may have had. Ask yourself: How did I respond?

- What behavior do I use when faced with conflict?

- What do I say and do when a conflict begins?

- Do I behave differently with different types of people?

- What behaviors have worked well for me and which have not been successful? Example: avoidance.

Another way to understand how you deal with conflict is to get feedback from other people. Ask your peers, your partner/spouse, your friends and family how they see you when responding to conflict.

To manage conflict effectively, control your emotions and respond empathetically. Empathy, the ability to understand and share the feelings of others, necessitates recognizing and comprehending our own emotions first. Empathy allows us to respond appropriately to situations. Empathy can be divided into three types:

Cognitive Empathy, also known as 'perspective-taking', is basically being able to put yourself into someone else's shoes and see things from their perspective.

Emotional Empathy, when you feel the other person's emotions with them, this is also known as 'emotional contagion.

Compassionate Empathy, having compassion and understanding of human nature, (feeling someone's pain and taking action to help resolve the issue).

Developing empathy starts with self-awareness of your own emotions and feelings. To better understand others and enhance empathy you must acknowledge various perspectives, ask questions, actively listen, reflect, and strive to understand the other person's viewpoint. Compassion and sincerity are also integral to the empathic process.

Self-Compassion and Setting Boundaries

In addition to extending compassion to others, it's equally important to practice self-compassion, which may entail setting boundaries in your relationships. Setting boundaries becomes a crucial component in maintaining healthy connections. If certain individuals repeatedly take advantage of your kindness, engage in harmful gossip, or cause emotional distress, it may be time to establish boundaries. Ask yourself:

- *Who are the people closest to me and how do they make me feel?*
- *Who allows me to be my authentic self?*
- *Who can I trust and be vulnerable with?*
- *How do I know I need to establish better boundaries?*
- *How do I define my boundaries?*

- How do I make others aware of the changes?

- Do I find it difficult to set boundaries?

- How do I maintain my boundaries?

Discern when to invest more or less in a relationship. Nurture connections with individuals who consistently support, encourage, and reciprocate your efforts, forming the foundation for meaningful relationships. It's important to remember that not all relationships will be deeply meaningful, and that's perfectly acceptable. Professional relationships, such as those with clients, often have a different dynamic than personal ones. The key is to cultivate connections with like-minded individuals who contribute positively to your life, bring you joy, and fill your emotional cup – this is your tribe.

Cultivating personal and meaningful relationships is an essential contributor to our mental and emotional well-being. These deep connections enrich our lives and contribute significantly to our overall life satisfaction and fulfillment. They serve as pillars of strength during challenging times, reminding us that we have a support system of people who genuinely care and love us. As life unfolds, people may come and go, but for those with whom we share deep and meaningful connections, their impact remains etched in our souls, leaving an indelible mark.

CHAPTER 16:

Work-Life Harmony

Chris Wilkinson

Work-life harmony is an upgrade on the outdated term *work-life balance*, which is analog. Linear. Arithmetic.

Work-life harmony is digital. Exponential. Work-life balance 2.0. Fluid and flexible. It requires the deliberate setting of boundaries, but *holding* those boundaries is where most fail.

Work-life harmony is about integration, prioritization with clarity, intention, and discipline. Communication with key stakeholders (like your spouse & kids). Adaptation. Nothing rigid like a '9 to 5'. It allows for an intermingling of work and personal priorities. It's a beautifully choreographed dance, and you are the choreographer.

Harmony implies synergy. Less about the classic give-and-take balance approach, it's a beautiful fusion of life's components to form a greater whole. Akin to the yin-yang symbol. A fluid and flexible mosaic that portrays a sense of seamless integration, like a conductor masterfully guiding an orchestral ensemble.

Why do you want more work-life harmony? Is it that you feel a disconnection? A misalignment in how your schedule, and your life is unfolding each day compared to how you envisioned it? Do you feel that uncomfortable energy in the pit of your stomach when things are quiet? Is it an uneasy tension that sits in your shoulders and neck? The unwelcome burst and need to last out or an inability to remain still for even 5 minutes? How is this impacting your work, your relationships, and your wellness?

This disillusionment does not have to be your legacy. This kind of inner anarchy that you feel in your gut has a solution. The answer is found in the work. The reflective, problem-solving work to find a better way forward.

Interestingly, it's this kind of pain of misalignment that inspires the greatest growth. And I want you to harness this misalignment, this discomfort, and USE IT! Channel it for even a few moments, and whenever you need it, then use its tension to catapult you forward with motivation to change.

What is it that you envision for yourself when you are in your best space? What does work-life harmony even look like? Your family, career, health & wellness, wealth-building, downtime, "me" time, outside interests, friends, holidays - all of it requires focus & attention.

Look, the truth is that no one can prescribe your work-life harmony to you. No one can tell you how much time each day you should dedicate to each of your most important priorities. Does your social media marketing deserve 30 minutes today? An hour? Two hours? Or making a sales call? Five minutes? Ten minutes? What if you're a driven person who wants to work more than your partner wants you to? Maybe you happen to love building your career! How do you handle this? I can understand if the idea of having to choose makes you uncomfortable.

You are going to win some days and lose others. The goal is to get many more wins! You win some days by striking the right mix of work, family, and "you" time. Then you lose some days by feeling like you didn't spend enough time with work, family, friends, "you time", or all of the above!

Here's the rub: it will never be perfect. Why? Because it's often your inner judge that holds the power over you as to whether it was the "right" mix. When your inner judge, which is tied to your ego, is holding your metaphorical steering wheel it means you are allowing it to control your thoughts and determine whether your work-life harmony is "good" or "bad". The judge just wants to be "right", and everything that doesn't serve our ego's desires it views as "wrong".

Stanford Lecturer and NY Times bestselling author, Shirzad Chamine, Ph.D., speaks to this in his book *Positive Intelligence.* It contains fascinating brain science and practical applications for all of us. According to the research, our inner judge overpowers us by telling us what is wrong with us, others, and/or the situation; it makes us feel inferior and "less than"; and then, it makes us feel negative and defeated by these same thoughts. What a double kick in the gut!

Work-Life Harmony Starts by Controlling Your Judge

If we are going to attack the root cause of work-life misalignment, the first step to genuine work-life harmony is controlling your inner judge, which is programmed to keep us safe by playing small. It may have served us when we were younger, in certain environments, but as an adult it's counterproductive to heed the judge's "play small" direction.

The judge is the voice that says you can't have work-life harmony. This voice that says work-life harmony is a myth is, ironically, the same voice that makes you feel bad for not having the work-life harmony that it just said doesn't exist. The judge is a liar.

The best ways to overcome the inner judge? Employing empathy (for self, as much as others), curiosity, purpose, and gratitude. Dr. Chamine strongly suggests a practice of focusing on what's going right, rather than what's going wrong.

Pro tip: A 1-minute Practice! Create a reminder in your smartphone or on your schedule a few times a day to remind yourself to listen for & dismiss the lies of the inner judge and, to instead, focus on what is going right! Also, practice a related gratitude in that moment to finish the 1-minute practice. Feel your gratitude in your upper abdomen & chest for maximum impact. Try it now!

Motivation + Clarity Leads to Aligned Intention

When you have the motivation for improvement, and you integrate it with clarity of purpose, you unleash the power of aligned intention.

Intention. Such a beautiful concept. No other word radiates such a deep understanding of inner alignment fused with powerful action. Alignment of deep purpose, core values, and engaging work create flow and remove tension. Intention is so impactful because it ties together the notions of one's powerful purpose, right aim, deliberate planning, and laser-focused goals – priming us for driven action.

When intention, aligned priorities, and driven action are present, high performance follows. Efficiency and harmony await.

In his popular book, *High Performance Habits*, acclaimed author & coach Brendon Burchard labels the six habits: seek clarity, generate energy, raise necessity, increase productivity, develop influence, and demonstrate courage.

Intention is explored by Burchard through his idea of "seeking clarity". In his best seller, he instructs us to be clear about what is most important. What is most meaningful in your life? How do you want to impact your life and others? What emotions do you want to experience more of? How do you want to show up in your life – as in, what values do you want to represent with your interactions and behaviours every day?

Pro Tip: It's best to journal on these questions and get clear answers on exactly what you want and how you want to show up. When you answer these questions for yourself, you will have aligned intentions. You will be able to answer the best question that has ever existed – 'What Do I Really Want?'

Removing Limiting Beliefs to Drive Aligned Action

Taking aligned action is as much about removing your limitations as it is moving forward. As much about removing the brakes as it is stepping on the gas.

When I was little, I remember my dad taking me to the go-karts for the first time. I was so excited! When it was time to throttle up and go, I recall being so excited I stepped on the gas and brake pedals as hard as I could at the same time. That go-kart engine revved right up, and I went nowhere! It's such an apt metaphor for how we go about our highest priorities. Much enthusiasm about moving ahead, yet with the brakes firmly locked on. In this metaphor, the brakes represent limiting beliefs.

Here is how to remove your brakes so you can put your beautiful intentions and aligned actions first. For this exercise, finish this sentence stem: "I am not as far ahead with my work-life harmony because: ..." Then whatever block you discover, ask yourself why that block is present.

For instance, if your answer to the first sentence stem was "because I let competing priorities win out for my time", then you ask yourself, "Why do I let competing priorities win out for my time?". Continue to ask yourself why at each answer until you can't go any deeper. At that point you will have the deeper reason you have been (unintentionally) keeping your foot on the brakes. It's incredibly empowering when you discover what's been holding you back. Then you must act.

Your Next 5 Moves

With motivation and clarity present, it becomes much easier to plan your next five moves. One of the worst feelings entrepreneurs deal with is the feeling that you're working incredibly hard, but not getting anywhere meaningful!

When strategizing, choose your next 5 steps that are aligned with where you want to go, aligned with the intentions you identified earlier in this chapter with your strategic planning sessions.

Next apply this "next 5 moves" concept at different scales. That is, what are your next 5 moves for each of your top goals for the year, quarter, month, and week? Where are they written down so you (and your team) can see them? Connect with these goals and steps each morning.

When coaching my small business clients, I ask to see their calendar early and often. It remains the best way to prove what's important to them and to see how affected by distractions they can be.

To be the efficient and productive high performer you envision with work-life harmony, you will need to be very deliberate in your approach. As Burchard explains in *High Performance Habits*, those who achieve higher and give themselves the best chance at work-life harmony identify with statements such as, "I'm good at setting priorities and working on what is important", and "I stay focused and avoid distractions and temptations".

This means saying "no" more often to hold your boundaries. One coaching friend of mine has had much success with setting boundaries around her work-life harmony. Her simple *'Four Quarters'* work-life harmony model goes like this: The first quarter of her day is for her self-care, exercise and mindset work ("me"). The second quarter of her day is focused on intentional planning and strategic thinking. The third quarter is for tactics and operations. And the fourth quarter is family time ("we"). It's simple and effective! Take what you want from this and make it yours.

As Warren Buffett once said, "The difference between successful people and really successful people is that really successful people say NO to almost everything."

Maintaining Energy

One of the secret weapons of highly productive, fulfilled, and energetic people is that they implement mental micro-breaks during their workday. Mental energy is more integral than physical energy to avoiding the evening crash. It often takes longer to replenish mental energy. Practicing mental energy conservation is key to maintaining work-life harmony.

Pro Tip: Give your brain a mental micro-break every 1-2 hours, for 1-2 minutes, by focusing on being present with your breathing. Take five slow, deep breaths and simply listen to your inflow and outflow. No checking news, social, or emails. A micro-break is exactly what the brain needs every hour or two to remain creative and energized.

What Gets Measured, Gets Done

Success is not just about managing time; it's about understanding and optimizing your energy. To build mental energy awareness, see patterns, and course correct when necessary – your energy must be tracked.

Pro Tip: Answer these questions each week:

1. *Out of 10 (10 = excellent and 1 = poor), how well did I execute on my work-life harmony?*

2. *What did I do well?*

3. *Where could I have done better?*

Track your answers every week. Your week isn't complete until you have briefly recorded your answers. Look for patterns and elevate your game with your own observations.

Lastly, Bring an Attitude of 'Play'

As with any work in progress, the first version of your work-life harmony won't be your Mona Lisa. Bring a spirit of playfulness and embrace this challenge with enthusiasm. With each refinement of your work-life harmony, fully indulge in the play and joy of it, letting that fuel each subsequent iteration.

I Celebrate You

As coaches we love the saying, "Celebrate to Integrate!". Celebrate your wins and new habits to fully integrate them by hacking your dopamine reward center. This will make you crave these new habits more powerfully and consistently.

A celebration to hack your reward centre can be as simple as a metaphorical pat on your own back, sharing a win with a friend, or treating yourself.

And when you want to, celebrate in even bigger ways! When you reach certain milestones, make sure to celebrate with friends. The kind of celebrations that create memories! Fun. Rewarding. Aligned with the person you are becoming even more proud of. Even more intentional. Even more harmonious.

Be the hero of your own story.

References

[1] Interpretations of Greek Mythology (Routledge Revivals). United Kingdom: Taylor & Francis, 2014.

[2] Radical Poetics and Secular Jewish Culture. United States: University of Alabama Press, 2010.

[3] Rumi, Mevlana Jalaluddin. The Rumi Collection: An Anthology of Translations of Mevlana Jalaluddin Rumi. United States: Shambhala, 2023.

[4] Brown, Brené. The Gifts of Imperfection: Let Go of Who You Think You're Supposed to Be and Embrace Who You Are. United States: Hazelden Publishing, 2022.

[5] Jung, Carl Gustav. The Archetypes and the Collective Unconscious. United Kingdom: Princeton University Press, 1969.

[6] Goleman, Daniel. Emotional Intelligence: Why It Can Matter More Than IQ. United Kingdom: Random House Publishing Group, 2012.

[7] Campbell, Joseph. The Hero with a Thousand Faces (Paladin Books). United Kingdom: Fontana, 1993.

[8] Robinson, Ken, and Lou Aronica. *The Element: How Finding Your Passion Changes Everything*. New York City, Random House, 2009, p. 255.

[9] MacMillan, Amanda. "4 Possible Reasons Why Mental Health Is Getting Worse." *Health*, Dotdash Meredith, 21 Aug. 2023, https://www.health.com/condition/depression/8-million-americans-psychological-distress. Accessed 24 Oct. 2023.

[10] Goleman, Daniel. *Emotional Intelligence*. Bantam Books trade paperback edition. ed., New York City, Bantam Books, 2020, p. 5.

[11] Kain Ramsay. "The Beautiful Attitudes of Effective Life Coaching" *Udemy* Udemy,

Inc. Jan 8, 2021. https://www.udemy.com/course/life-coaching-online-certification-course-life-coach-training/learn/lecture/ 14099968#overview Oct 24, 2023.

[12] Thomas Jefferson, et al. *Declaration of Independence* 07-04-1776. National
 Archives Museum, Washington DC. Manuscript/Mixed Material

[13] Murgaš, František, et al. "Happiness or Quality of Life? Or Both?" *Journal of Education Culture and Society*, vol. 13, no. 1, 30 June 2022,
https://jecs.pl/index.php/jecs/article/view/1408. Accessed 25 Oct. 2023.

[14] Suttie, Jill. "Why Americans Struggle to be Happy." *Greater Good Magazine*, 26
 Oct. 2015, greatergood.berkeley.edu/article/item/
 why_americans_struggle_to_be_happy. Accessed 24 Oct. 2023.

[15] Friedman, Kinky. *Cowboy Logic: The Wit and Wisdom of Kinky Friedman (and Some of His Friends)*. New York City, St. Martin's Griffin, 2007.

[16] Tolle, Eckhart. *The Power of Now: A Guide to Spiritual Enlightenment*. Sydney,
Hachette Australia, 2011, p. 146.

[17] Frankl, Viktor E., et al. *Man's Search for Meaning*. Boston, Beacon Press, 2014, p. 144.

[18] Frankl, p. 77, 114, 144.

[19] Frankl, p. 110.

[20] Goleman, p. 34

[21] Goleman, p. 34

[22] Rogers, Carl R. *On Becoming a Person: A Therapist's View of Psychotherapy*.
 London, Robinson, 2020, p. 351

[23] Lieberman, David J. *Never Get Angry Again: The Foolproof Way to Stay Calm and in Control in Any Conversation or Situation*. New York City, St. Martin's Press, 2019, p. 60

[24] Goleman, p. xv; 24.

[25] Robinson, p. 22-24, 151.

[26] Goleman, p. 36.

[27] Goleman, p. 9.

[28] Goleman, p. 41.

[29] Goleman, p. xv.

[30] Goleman, p. xxiii.

[31] Egan, Gerard, and Robert J. Reese. *The Skilled Helper: A Problem-Management and Opportunity-Development Approach to Helping*. 11th ed., Cengage, 2022, p. 46, 67.

[32] Goleman, p. 150.

[33] Peirce, Penney. *Frequency: The Power of Personal Vibration*. New York City, Atria Books, 2011, p. 112.

[34] Egan, p. 12, 16.

[35] Robinson, p. 160.

[36] Robinson, p. 9.

[37] Robinson, p. 38-42.

[38] Robinson, p. 36.

[39] Robinson, p. 49-50.

[40] Robinson, p. 57.

[41] Robinson, p. 56-57.

[42] Robinson, p. 93.

[43] Robinson, p. 92.

[44] Robinson, p. 93, 96.

[45] Robinson, p. 136.

[46] Robinson, p. 136.

[47] Robinson p. 202.

[48] Robinson p. 195.

[49] Robinson p. 195

[50] Moore, Catherine. "What is Eudaimonia? Aristotle and Eudaimonic Wellbeing."
Positive Psychology, PositivePsychology.com B.V., 8 Apr. 2019, positivepsychology.com/eudaimonia/. Accessed 27 Oct. 2023.

[51] Moore.

Printed by Amazon Italia Logistica S.r.l.
Torrazza Piemonte (TO), Italy

59327475R00131